Give me This Mountain!

Caleb said, "Now, I am old,
but as yet I am as strong this day as I was;
as my strength was then, even so is my strength now,
for war, both to go out, and to come in.

Now, therefore, ***give me this mountain***
of which the Lord spoke in that day."

Joshua 14:10-12

God Bless
Don Schroder

by

Don Schroder

Promise Pubishing Co.  Orange, CA, 92665

Give Me This Mountain!

Orange CA 92865

Edited by M. B. Steele

Printed in the United States of America

Library of Congress Cataloging-in-Publication

Schroder, Don
Give me This Mountain!

ISBN 0-939497-44-1

ABOUT THE AUTHOR

Don Schroder was born and reared in St. John, Kansas. He attended church during his childhood and youth, but he did not know what it was to be a true believer in Christ until he was in the U. S. Air Force. While serving in Japan, Don accepted the Lord under the ministry of a missionary who ministered to servicemen. Later, he was baptized in Tokyo Bay. Don then began working with a missionary known as Pop Ross, distributing tracts and holding street meetings. It was at that time that the Lord spoke to Don about serving Him fulltime on the mission field.

After the Korean war, Don returned to the States and attended Midwest Bible College (now Calvary Bible College), in Kansas City, MO, earning a B. A. degree. During his third year in Bible college, he felt called to serve the Lord in South America. In December of 1960, Don, his wife, Monnie, and their children began their ministry in Ecuador with Radio Station HCJB.

Don had known the printing business since the age of twelve and was qualified to serve as Director of the HCJB print shop where he served for 23 years. The shop printed hundreds of thousands of pieces of literature in 17 different languages.

HCJB, the Voice of the Andes, is owned and operated by World Radio Missionary Fellowship, Inc., a non-profit, non-commercial interdenominational organization dedicated to *Heralding Christ Jesus' Blessing* to all the world via the many ministries God has given them. Founded in 1931, HCJB was the world's first missionary radio station.

In addition to the print shop ministry, Don became involved in Indian evangelism and helped to establish many churches among the Quichua Indians living in the mountains of Ecuador. He also served in various ministries among the Indians in the jungles of Ecuador.

In addition to ministry in Central America, South America, and North America, Don and his wife, Monnie, have also ministered in Europe, Asia, Australia and New Zealand. They now live in Arkansas and travel throughout the United States on behalf of HCJB—World Radio Missionary Fellowship.

FOREWORD

I enjoyed the opportunity of reading the manuscript of Don Schroder's book. I was eyewitness to many of the experiences which Don describes, and you can be assured that this account tells it like it was.

Don and his family, along with their colleagues, perseveringly participated in rugged work and witness. They "... endured hardness as good soldiers of Jesus Christ." The Lord brought abundant fruit as a result.

The story deals with two amazing events—first was the building of the Loreto dam. Don and his helpers accomplished this with very limited physical resources and in the face of fierce obstacles. By the Lord's power, they achieved great and mighty things.

The second event was the amazing explosion of the gospel power among the Quichua Indians. Many factors contributed. The Lord answered the prayers of many who had lifted their hearts to Him through the years for these isolated people whom time had passed by. Prayer results in effective work, and Don Schroder has excelled in diligent service among the Quichuas. We commend him and we thank the Lord.

I'm sure that this true narrative will inspire and refresh you. Then, read, enjoy and serve the Lord with gladness.

Dr. Abe C. Van Der Puy

President Emeritus, HCJB World Radio

DEDICATION

To my wife, Monnie, for her faithful devotion to the Lord, to me and to our work in Ecuador. She made my work much easier by her sacrificial dedication to our home and family. Without her unwavering support, this entire project would have been greatly hindered.

To my sister, Ruth Lee, for her hours of work and research in organizing the sequence of events for this book.

To all our supporting churches and individuals who, *through their faithful gifts and prayers*, made this ministry possible.

Table of Contents

PREFACE

The construction of the Loreto Dam was the work of God using human instrumentalities blessed and guided by Him ..., as were the events that followed. While reading the account of these adventures which relates events as they unfolded, please remember my total dependency on divine providence.

This is what happened as seen through the eyes of an average guy with no special talent, but with a willingness to be used of God.

This account deals with the story from a human perspective of the problems, solutions, dangers, victories, joys and hardships. While God is not mentioned in regard to each day's activities, He undergirded and oversaw the entire project and ministry, and glory should be given to Him alone.

Yours In Christ,

Don Schroder

Chapter 1

Being in the Way, the Lord Led Me

For two long days, our small band of men and animals set our faces into the wind, rain and snow. The rain made the trail slick and muddy, and the horses often struggled clumsily, trying to stay on their feet. At times, we reached altitudes of up to 15,000 feet as we made our way across the top of the barren Andes mountains. The cold and damp hugged our weary bodies without any let-up. The elements were not only ever-present, they soaked into our bones making the thought of ever being warm again seem like an impossible dream. We found no refuge from them.

Suddenly, we stood before the great valley where those gigantic mountains drop off toward the jungles of the Amazon Valley. Wispy clouds floated past us far below our lofty point as we stood gazing at the lush beauty of this unspoiled land. From the austerity and starkness of the mountains so far above the tree line, we looked down at the tangled growth of the jungle, knowing the heat and humidity far below us was as wearing as the cold was at our high perch.

The valley stretched out below us fading into the distance while high mountains stood guard on three sides. Nestled there ... somewhere ... lay a small Indian village called Oyacachi. The Quichua Indian guides said this village was made up of fugitives from the law; the guides refused to go near the place. They told stories of having been shot at while trying to fish in the river that winds through the valley.

We had come to tell these people about Christ and His love, though, and we pushed through the emotional barriers, just as we had pushed through the physical barriers. We could not turn back.

Finally, one Indian agreed to go with me into the village in spite of the fact that these people had never before been visited by missionaries. The village was nearly impossible to reach. Few people even knew it existed.

Fearing the worst, the other two guides offered nothing more than, "We will wait here in the mountains until tomorrow morning."

I replied, "If we are not back by ten o'clock tomorrow morning go for help."

We had no idea what kind of reception to expect. As we made our way down the steep mountainside, the tension of the unknown coupled with the physical hardships overwhelmed us as did those beautiful, ominous mountains. Our eyes were often filled with the grandeur of such high peaks wearing their mantles of snow, gleaming and reflecting the sun in magnificent display. However, we had also visited the muddy villages where people live in the depths of degradation, finding solace only in the liquor which sends the entire village into a stupor each weekend. Life was not kind in these mountains. We knew it could bring out the worst in those who suffered in its grip.

We had to walk the horses back and forth in a zig-zag pattern along the side of the mountain, mostly cutting our own trail, descending only a little bit at a time so the horses wouldn't lose their footing and roll all the way to the bottom. There was no safety rail to stop them if they rolled down that steep mountainside. They would surely be killed.

Eventually we reached the river, glad for the change of angle after so long a time working our way downward on the steep trail. There we found a small trail leading into the village, but the village itself was still several miles away. We embarked on the trail with a certain amount of fear and uncertainty. To us, the village was "the unknown", but we knew God had led us to this village and we were in His hands. We comforted ourselves with that.

At long last, our demanding trek came to an end. We saw some Indians standing in the middle of the trail about two or three hundred yards in front of us.

My thoughts travelled to the Bible story of Abraham's servant who was sent to find a bride for Isaac. He started out, not knowing where he was going or who he was to choose for Isaac's bride. He made that long trek knowing that he was entirely dependent on God's willingness to direct him. Without that, his efforts would be in vain. Yet, he journeyed toward Abraham's relatives, asking for God's guidance. When he found Rebekah, he believed that God had led him. He thanked the God of Abraham, saying, "I being in the way, the Lord led me ...."

Like Abraham's servant, I started out to make contact with someone (I didn't know who) in a distant place, with little announcement of my coming, and I had no idea what kind of reception I would receive. I could only trust the Lord to lead me.

As we stood there, I thought, "What now?"

I also asked myself, "How did I get into this?"

Good question!

* *

Way back in 1931, Dr. Clarence Jones and Dr. Reuben Larson started a radio station near the equator, high in the Andes mountains. Dr. Jones had a vision to reach the *world* by radio, and his sketchy information included the fact that the equator was the best place to undertake such a feat. He also knew that a granite mountain is one of the best "sounding boards" in the world for radio. In his searching, he found Ecuador, South America, and he settled in the capital city of Quito. There on one of the largest granite mountain ranges in the world, located just ten miles south of the line of the equator, sits this ancient city occupied by the Inca Indians in past centuries. There, nearly 10,000 feet high in the mountains (that's almost two miles high), Clarence Jones and Reuben Larson found their hoped-for site where radio transmitters could reach to nearly every part of the globe.

Ecuador (Spanish for equator) is a small country, roughly the size of the state of Colorado. It straddles the equator in the northwest corner of South America. It is bounded on the north by Columbia, on the south and east by Peru and on the west by the Pacific Ocean.

The Andes Mountains, the longest mountain chain in the world, runs north and south, cutting the country of Ecuador almost in half. The mountains march up from Chile through Peru sometimes in a single line and sometimes dividing into double file. Where they are in pairs, elevated plains and plateaus are formed between the eastern and western mountains. These mountains are the backbone of South America, strung along the west coast. Nowhere else in the world are there so many peaks of such great height forming a chain of mountains.

In the southern part of Ecuador, Mount Chimborazo is nearly 22,000 feet high with a snowline at 15,000 feet. It is the tallest volcanic mountain in the world and is always snow-capped. Mount Cotopaxi, also in the southern part of Ecuador, is the tallest *active volcano* in the world. It is also eternally snow-capped and rises to 17,500 feet. The Quichua Indians live in these mountains as high up as 14,000 feet. All these mountains have dirt covering the rock and this creates problems with land slides during the wet or rainy season.

The water that runs off the eastern slopes of the Andes Mountains eventually reaches the Amazon River. These waters are called the headwaters of the mighty Amazon. Tributaries of the Napo River (Ecuador's largest river) flow from these mountains through the jungles of Ecuador to reach the Amazon River in Brazil. Then, they flow another 2,000 miles to reach the Atlantic Ocean.

Because most of Ecuador is located high in the mountains, only part of it is jungle even though it sits right on the equator. Most of the jungles are in the interior—on the lower east side of the mountains. On the west side are equatorial coastal lowlands bordering the Pacific Ocean with many areas of jungle growth as well as flat, sandy areas.

There are over nine million people in Ecuador, mostly in the cities. More than a third of the population descended from the ancient Incas—the original Indian inhabitants of Ecuador. Today's decendents of the Incas—pure-blooded Indians—are called Quichuas. Others of the population include people of mixed Indian and Spanish origin. About one percent are pure Spanish.

With the conquest by the Spaniards in the 1500's came the influence of the State church which is still felt in modern times. In the 1500's, the church leaders declared that the Incas did not have a soul and could be killed at will, or used as beasts of burden. That attitude can still be found today among people of Spanish descent. As a result of this oppression, most of the Indians escaped to the high mountains to live; a few fled into the jungle. Their direct descendants are the ones who still live there today.

It was to this mountain home that Dr. Jones and Reuben Larson came to build their radio station.

* * * * * * * * * * * * * * * * * * * *

Christmas Day, 1931, was the day chosen for Dr. Jones and Reuben Larson to go on the air with 250 watts of power. This barely reached the limits of the city; they certainly did not reach the world! They had a potential audience of just six radio receivers in the entire country of Ecuador. They were men of vision, however, and they believed God's calling would become reality—in His own way and in His own time. Their vision was to reach the world with the gospel by radio, and by faith they called their undertaking, The World Radio Missionary Fellowship.

Years passed, but steadily this humble beginning became a megaphone for God broadcasting the gospel to the entire world by shortwave and satellite. The voice of The World Radio Missionary Fellowship reaches approximately eighty per cent of the land mass of the world by shortwave, in numerous languages, so people everywhere can hear the gospel message in their own tongue. Truly this is a magnificent work of God!

Through the years many missionaries have been called by God to put their shoulder to the wheel to make this happen. Some have given their entire lives in Quito with only heaven knowing who heard their voices and the message of the Gospel. Few who hear have the ability or the means to make contact with the missionaries. They have been transplanted into the barren valley which sits high in the mountains, to that ancient city which has survived the invasion of armies and the inhospitality of nature. Still, the response these dedicated servants of the Lord get by way of the mails, thrills and motivates them to give this huge challenge all they've got and to wait for God to give the increase. They are soldiers of Christ, for sure!

Monnie and I shared their vision and for many years served alongside these warriors. I worked in the print shop, plying the trade I learned in my youth. Only heaven will reveal *where* that literature travelled - *which* hearts were warmed by the message of salvation and forgiveness - *who* found a Savior in Christ who no longer hung on a Cross in agony, but is now risen from the grave and alive. Their avid interest when we distributed tracts among those dark, vibrant people gave us a clue that many would read what we gave them with great interest. God has done the rest according to His plan.

Monnie faithfully cared for our family and many others who needed her energy, quiet strength and vital interest in the people who surrounded her. You seldom found her alone. She ministered to one and all who came to our home, to the missionary compound and to the hospital which was part of the mission's service to the people of Ecuador. She was a beautiful picture of God's love expressed by the labors of her hands in caring for others.

Our life as missionaries was not exactly exciting, but we always had the sense that we were doing something worthwhile with our lives. Only sometimes when we heard of the adventures of pioneering missionaries, we felt our service was pretty hum-drum. We just knew that our jobs needed to be done and we were willing to do them. We contented ourselves with the confidence that we were doing God's will—that was enough.

Chapter 2

Ignorance is Bliss

In the early 1960's, HCJB bought the water rights to Lake Loreto from the Ecuadorian government. This lake is located high in the Andes mountains east of Quito on the far side of the Continental Divide. There, the rainy season is timed to be opposite the rainy season on the western slopes. There was hope that somehow this lake could help provide electricity to drive the huge generators powering the massive signal that The World Radio Missionary Fellowship sent around the world by then. The purchase included the entire watershed slopes, the water which drained into and flowed out of the lake. These are the actual headwaters of the Amazon river which gathers many tributaries into its grip as it flows eastward into the Atlantic Ocean.

For the first thirty years of the operation of the radio ministry, electricity had been supplied by large diesel generators. But by 1960, diesel fuel had become too expensive to use so, since we had purchased water rights, our first hydroelectric plant was built far below Lake Loreto in the small native village of Papallacta. Over the next several years, a study was made and it was found that for about twenty-one days every year, the water level of the lake dropped too low to adequately supply the needed electricity. Power from the new hydro-plant was greatly reduced for those periods, thereby limiting the reach of the radio station signal.

HCJB engineers working with this water problem came up with the idea that if they could go east of Quito, to Lake Loreto and build a dam there, enough water might be preserved during the rainy season to be released during the dry season to provide an uninterrupted production of electricity for HCJB. The lake was almost inaccessible, but it was about one-and-a-half miles long, big enough to hold the precious water we needed.

With this in mind, the engineers decided to go to the lake and measure to see if their idea really could produce the desired results. If feasible, they could then formulate plans to carry out the building of a dam. They asked if I would like to accompany them. I was surprised to be asked to go since I'm not an engineer, but nevertheless, I was intrigued and quickly accepted the invitation without hesitation. There was only one reason I could ever come up with as to why I was asked to go along with the engineers: As far as I know, I was the only man at HCJB who owned a little rubber boat—at least as far as we knew. Having no engineering knowledge or skills whatsoever, I knew of no other reason to be included.

To reach our destination at Lake Loreto was no simple task. It was not just a matter of hopping into a car and driving to the lake. Such a trip demands a really good reason for going—it isn't just a nice backpacking jaunt through the forest. It is a potentially life-threatening experience which drains the strongest man and challenges his limits. Still, I was intrigued and glad to be included.

Very early on the morning of the appointed day, we gathered in the pouring rain, three engineers and myself along with four Quichua Indians to carry the boat and equipment. We left Quito in a Land Rover, travelling to the top of the mountain pass. There, after two hours of bouncing over cobblestone roads, we had to leave the Land Rover at the end of the paved road and walk the remainder of the way. From the road, it was a brisk six-hour walk to Lake Loreto.

This hike to the lake was up a towering mountain, down to a hidden valley, up another mountain, down to another valley—a pattern repeated several times. Then, when we thought we had just about made it to the lake, there before us was another huge mountain. We had no choice but to go forward. When we got to the top of that mountain after walking five-and-a-half hours, I thought, "All right! Now we can enter this little valley and we'll be there."

To my dismay when we got over the ridge there was another mountain and I groaned to myself, "Oh, no, I just can't make it!" My masculine pride is the only thing that kept my mouth shut. That ridge, to this day, is called "Heartbreak Ridge" because it almost breaks your heart to see yet another mountain before you when you have already walked so far, not to mention that you are bone-tired from the unaccustomed effort, cold from the altitude ... and wet from the persistent rain.

We finally made it over Heartbreak Ridge at about five o'clock in the evening and found Lake Loreto. By six o'clock it was very dark. Since it was still raining, we hurriedly set up our tents, took off our wet clothing and crawled into our sleeping bags. I for one was so cold, I could not stop shaking. After warming up a little, we got up and prepared our soup which warmed us some from the inside. We had no trouble sleeping. We were all exhausted from the long walk across the rugged mountains.

The next morning, the engineers busied themselves setting up their surveying instruments on the shore and determining a reference point across the lake. One of the engineers and I went out on the lake in my little rubber boat which was actually a two-man life boat. Measuring for depth was done by tying knots in a rope which was attached to an anchor. This anchor was dropped overboard, all the way to the bottom of the lake. In this way, the depth of different areas of the lake was determined as we moved back and forth across the lake. After one full day of work on the lake, the engineers had the information that they needed. All we had to do now was to get back to Quito. That thought was not pleasant as we contemplated that long, hard walk back to the Land Rover.

When the engineers got back to Quito and calculated the results, they knew just exactly what the bottom of the lake actually looked like. The engineers measured how much water was in the lake and they calculated how much they would have to raise the level of the lake in order to gain the water they needed to operate the hydroelectric plant. After all this measuring and calculating, they pretty well knew what was needed to utilize the waters of Lake Loreto.

Their plan was to construct an earth-filled dam and to build a construction road in to the site from the main road in order to transport the equipment and supplies necessary for building the dam. At that point, my contribution to the project had been made. I had furnished the boat and was now totally out of the picture. I went back to my job of running the print shop and had become nothing more than an interested bystander.

The engineers carefully studied all the possibilities and decided that it simply wasn't practical to build an access road to Lake Loreto. The terrain was exceptionally mountainous and marshy and they knew that it would cost more to build the road than to build the dam itself. They were ready to give up on the entire project—it seemed impossible, too expensive to be feasible.

I was still interested, I found, so I talked to Fred Woodburn, who was Director of Engineering at that time, and we discussed the possibility of building the dam by hand. Since a road couldn't be built economically to transport the needed construction equipment, it was the only other alternative. Fred had never been to the site, but I told him that I really thought it could be done. We hesitantly suggested the idea to the engineers.

The engineers were divided in their reaction. Some said it simply could not be done and some conceded that "... it might be possible." It was really a moot question, however, because there was no one who could or would head up the project. The idea wouldn't let go of me, however.

I felt akin to Caleb who spoke to Joshua *after* the Children of Israel had finished wandering in the desert for forty years. Caleb reminded Joshua that they had made the unpopular recommendation that the Children of Israel enter the Promised Land then. When they were outvoted and the Israelties decided not to go into the Land, Moses promised Caleb that he could have the land he had walked on for his inheritance. It turned out that his land was the well-fortified, mountainous area known as Hebron today. Even though Caleb was no longer a young man, he wanted that difficult task—he wanted what God had given him. He said, "Give me this mountain! If the Lord will be with me, then I will be able to drive the enemy out, as the Lord said."

Just so, I (with no experience in engineering and absolutely no experience in building dams) volunteered to head up the project to build an earth-filled dam by hand! My fellow missionaries must have thought I'd taken leave of my senses. But after all, being a printer, I figured that anyone could build a dam. I felt that I would be able to organize both the men and the actual work of building the dam, if they would tell me how to go about it. The engineers took me up on my offer! I became a dam builder! Of course, in Christian circles, we do not call it a dam; we call it a "water holder backer."

Chapter 3

Always Prepare

We all know that the Boy Scouts for many years have had the slogan, "Always Be Prepared" and it is a good philosophy. However, the words of a missionary lady I heard speak long ago still ring in my ears. She said that if we have ten years to serve the Lord, we should spend nine of those years in preparation and the last year in action. She was encouraging young people to train for the ministry or missionary service to which they felt called, and I'm not sure we should always go that far. Still, her words add up to, "Always Prepare" and I've found that helpful advice in my life. Nevertheless, nothing could have prepared me fully for what I was about to undertake.

The challenge was much greater than I anticipated—that's a nice way to say that I had no idea what I was up against. At an altitude of nearly 14,000 feet, the continual wind, rain and cold were worse than I could imagine. At night, the temperature went down to twenty degrees and the days possibly got up into the 70's at the most. On occasion, it snowed, but it always melted the next day. During the eleven months I worked on the dam, it rained all but six days.

Sometimes it rained all day long. Other times it rained just a little bit. It made the working conditions more than difficult. The Quichua Indians were the only ones who could take the extreme cold and rain. They had been raised at these altitudes in the Andes mountains and were accustomed to the harsh weather.

The coldest part of the year is June, July and August. During this season, it rains very hard almost all the time and the wind blows a gale, making it impossible to work until it breaks. We found that even during the "dry season", the rain and sleet (the Indians call it *papa cara*) came down so hard that the horses wouldn't walk into it because of its sting on their face and eyes. Imagine trying to ride a horse for six hours under these conditions.

At times the fog was so thick you couldn't see the trail in front of your nose. The Indians pretty well knew their way through the mountains, but sometimes even they got disoriented in the fog. The Indians told me, "When the fog rolls in, you must stop and wait until you can find a point of reference. Otherwise, you will wander around like a blind man."

The summer season basically lasts from October through March, so the building of the dam had to be done during those months.

Imagine, if you can, trying to plan the establishment of a camp site for yourself and dozens of workers at an altitude of nearly 14,000 feet. After making the two-hour trip by truck, we had a six-hour trip by foot into the dam site. All of this was carried out over some of the highest mountains of Ecuador, some of the highest in the world. Then in the valleys, we found marshland where the horses sometimes sank into the mud up to their bellies. The obstacles we faced were extremely difficult.

Everything we needed to start the camp had to be carried on our backs or packed in by mule or horseback. I had to plan housing for the many workers and figure out how to get enough food into the dam site to feed them. I had to find cooks to prepare the food. We needed a safe water supply to prevent sickness. We had to put in a sanitary system. We needed a supply of first-aid medicine in case of an accident or sickness. We had to purchase a boat and a motor to get the men and supplies across to the other side of the lake where the work must take place. I had to do all this before we could ever start digging the test holes and looking for clay.

This meant I had to do a lot of planning and organizing before we ever left Quito. I designed a pre-fab cabin out of plywood for myself, to be erected later at the dam site. Everything had to be cut so it would fit on the side of a mule. The largest piece of plywood could not be larger than two feet by four feet. The corrugated tin roof had to be rolled up and hand carried into the site since it was too long for the mules. The two-by-four-inch studs and flooring also had to be hand carried into the site.

All of this had to be exact and prepared ahead of time. Once I arrived at the site, there was no opportunity to make changes to anything on the cabin, so it had to be right. Two bench-like frames were also pre-fabricated to be used as beds. Foam rubber was placed on the frames, and they made a very comfortable bed. We constructed four boxes, 48 inches long by 24 inches wide by 18 inches high. These were to be used for carrying food to the site. One mule could carry two of these boxes if the weight was 100 pounds or less. I designed a special box with styrofoam on the inside to carry fresh eggs. Each box held 24 dozen eggs. These boxes were tied, one on each side of the mule, and carried to the dam site.

We also pre-fabricated a four-seat "outhouse" toilet. We put together a water system so we could have running water in the kitchen and in my cabin. I purchased some iron rods to be placed on rocks to serve as our stove. We cut fire wood for cooking at the site. I purchased a 12-foot aluminum boat and a ten-horsepower outboard motor to move the supplies and men across the lake. We purchased picks, shovels, pots and pans, a chainsaw and other small tools to be taken to the site.

I needed someone in Quito to do all the purchasing of food and supplies while I was at the lake. For the first five months, my wife, Monnie, took on that job while also taking care of our four children. She was also in charge of all the housekeeping at

HCJB's Voz Andes hospital in Quito. She played a really vital part in the dam project.

I arranged for HCJB's maintenance man, Roberto Coello, to deliver all the supplies to a point on the road called, *Penas Blancas* or White Cliffs, where the trail to the lake started. I had some Indians build a small hut at *Penas Blancas* to store the supplies and so that the muleskinners would have a place to sleep and cook. The supplies were taken to the hut each day by Roberto, and the muleskinners took them to the lake the next day.

As you can see, there were a lot of details to be taken care of before we ever left for the lake. Of course, all these supplies could not be taken in the first day. I had to determine what was the most critical for the first day and prioritize the goods for each day thereafter. Now that the supply line was set in place, supplies were purchased and Indian workers were hired, and we were ready to leave for the lake ... at last.

Because the cold, wet winters (summertime in North America) made it impossible for us to work at that altitude, we had to plan the work on the dam in two phases, both of which took place during the summer months (winter in North America). The first phase started in November, 1969, and lasted five months. The second phase started in September of 1970 and lasted until the completion of the dam. During the first phase, we planned to set up the camp, build a good trail for the horses and mules, dig test holes and look for the clay needed for the dam.

On November 10, 1969 at 4:00 in the morning, I left Quito in the company of Enoch Sanford, a missionary colleague. Enoch went to help me set up my pre-fab house. We left Quito in a pickup truck packed with food, sleeping bags, the boat and motor, and other supplies. At HCJB's transmitter site in Pifo, we picked up twelve workers. I had arranged for a muleskinner with six mules and two riding horses to meet us at *Penas Blancas*. The muleskinners had arrived the day before and spent the night in the little hut we had built for them. They would make a daily trip into the lake. We arrived at *Penas Blancas* about 8:00 that morning, and ten of the men started into the lake on foot, carrying the boat. The supplies from the pickup were loaded onto the pack horses. At about 9:30, Enoch and I, both on horseback, left for the lake with the pack horses.

The pack horses had a bad time on the rough terrain. One horse almost went over a cliff and we all thought he was lost. He turned just in time and instead of going over the cliff, he came skidding down the hill on his haunches, sliding right through the place where we were all sitting, having our noon meal. Needless to say, we scattered in every direction in our effort to escape his passage through the middle of our lunch.

Pack Horses on Their Way to Loreto

One of the horses got stuck in the mud and had to be unloaded and pulled out. Usually the horses get stuck by getting into one of the bogs and their legs sink down into the mud until their stomachs are resting on the surface. They can't get any footing to get themselves out, so they have to be unloaded and pyhsically pulled out of the bog. The Indians have a rather primitive, but effective, method of getting the horse to cooperate in getting himself out. One Indian pulls up on the horse's tail while another one pulls on the halter. This tail pulling stimulates the horse to struggle and eventually they are able to pull him out.

Another horse couldn't make it up a steep incline and had to be unloaded. The rest of the horses were pushed up the hill. Eventually, they all made it.

We finally arrived at the lake around four o'clock in the afternoon. Hastily, we put the boat into the water and were ready to take the first group across to the designated camp site, when it started raining a virtual downpour! We unloaded the horses in the drenching rain and sent them back for more supplies. I made seven round trips across the lake and back in the boat that first day, in the pouring rain. There was no choice but to get all the supplies across the lake.

We had to bring all the equipment and supplies across the lake in the boat. A horse couldn't get to the head of the lake because of the cliffs and the marshland. The lake walls went almost straight up on three sides since Loreto is a volcano crater lake. A trail had to be cut down the mountainside in a zig-zag pattern on the backside of the lake and then across some marshy land along the lakeside.

The front of the lake where the river flowed out was designated for the camp site and the dam site. Quichua Indians had built two small huts at the lower end of the lake to keep dry when they came up to the lake to fish. The huts were in bad repair and we had to put a tarp over our heads to keep the rain off while we tried to sleep. The earthen floor was bumpy and uneven. Our first night was not a good night to put it mildly.

The next day Enoch and I tried to dry out our wet sleeping bags over an open fire. We split some large plastic bags and put them on the roof until the Indians could patch it with Paramo grass (a wiry, tough grass that grows in the high mountainous regions). The Indians cut grass and spread it over the floor to make it more comfortable for sleeping. We drove nails into some of the supports so we could hang up our clothes. With all these comforts it seemed almost like home (well, *almost*). We had no heat of any kind in our little hut and trying to dry our clothes and bedding was a constant, but necessary, battle.

Don in Front of His First Hut in Lake Loreto

The Indians slept in another thatched-roof hut, larger than ours. The cooking was done in their hut, so we spent a lot of time around the open fire in their hut.

Segundo Bustamante, my foreman, had some of the men hard at work on the trail. The rest of the men were clearing the area where the permanent buildings would be erected. We needed one large thatched-roof hut for the kitchen and dining room and another where the workers could sleep. These had to be large enough to accommodate over one hundred workers.

We also needed a thatched-roof hut for storage of equipment. After the site was cleared for my house, Enoch and I cut down what passes for trees at these extreme altitudes (just knotty sticks, unlike what is normally thought of as trees). We cut them into stumps about twelve inches long. Dozens of them had to be cut. We placed these on the leveled ground to form the foundation for the pre-fab house. We sank the stumps into the ground so that the tops were all perfectly level, about eight inches high. We erected the house on these stumps, leaving an air space of about eight inches. It was like a house sitting on short stilts.

Don Cutting Stumps for the Foundation of His House

At the same time, we had horses and mules bringing in all the parts of the pre-fab house. The corrugated tin for the roof was carried in by hand. Other supplies were brought in at the same time. All these things had to be brought across the lake by boat.

We also had men digging test holes, looking for clay for the earth-filled dam. The Lake was a beehive of activity with many things going on at the same time.

I had no way to communicate with the outside world during that time. So, once a week, I sent a letter to Monnie with a list of supplies we needed. An Indian carried these letters and lists across the mountains to Monnie in Quito. She went to the market and purchased everything on the list and gave it to Roberto. Roberto purchased the larger items such as lumber, hardware and the steel barrels we needed. He then packed everything up in the truck and took it to the little hut at *Penas Blancas* and left it there for the muleskinners to take into the lake.

Once a month, I left Lake Loreto and spent four days in Quito with Monnie and the children. That was always a special time. I had to ride a horse six hours to *Penas Blancas*. Roberto met me there and took me to Quito by truck. In all, it took me eight hours of travelling to get home. Monnie always had my favorite meal ready when I got home and a delicious pie for me to eat. I lived like a king for those four days and it was hard to leave my family to go back to the lake.

Once all the parts to the pre-fab house were at the lake, Enoch and I started putting it together. It was quite a job to assemble it, but once it was up, we could finally stay dry. Enoch returned to Quito after the little cabin was completed. He helped me out for about a month. I had no heat in my little cabin so I purchased an old oil heater from Quito. I installed it in the cabin, but I still don't know if it was a blessing or a curse. The thing smoked most of the time and I almost had to sit on top of it to get warm. I guess it was better than nothing. It kept me humble (we all need that).

I installed the water system in my cabin and in the kitchen. Two fifty-gallon steel barrels were carried in by mule, one on each side. The barrels had removable tops so we could check the water level. These barrels were set on a high platform so that gravity could provide water pressure. The barrels were equipped with two faucets at the bottom. A pipe was run between the two barrels at the bottom, so the water level of both barrels stayed the same at all time, giving us even better water pressure. From one faucet, a hose was run to the kitchen. From the other faucet, a hose was run to my cabin. Faucets were attached to the end of the hoses, and we had running water! I installed an old sink in my cabin to use as a washbasin. The drain just went through the floor and into the ground under the cabin.

Don With His Water System and His House

A much larger hose was taken out into the lake, fifteen or twenty yards from shore, and dropped down into the water about three feet. This was to ensure that we pumped fresh clean water out of the lake. I put a weight on the end of the hose and a float at water level. Another weight was attached which dropped all the way to the bottom of the lake, acting as an anchor, so the hose was stationary and did not move about. I purchased a hand pump and hooked it up between the hose running to the barrels and the one coming out of the lake. Every day I sent a man down to the lake, and he pumped water until the barrels were full.

I realized, of course, with so many men there was a need for a latrine. I used my experience gained in the Air Force. I had the latrine built on the other side of the ridge near the camp so the waste water and drainage would not run back into the lake when it rained. So the "four-holer" outhouse was built. Wooden steps were constructed, making it easier to climb the hill. What I did not realize was that the Indians had no idea what an outhouse was and they had no idea how to use one. I had to educate them on the health benefits of an outhouse. Then I tried to convince them they must all use the outhouse. They were accustomed to just relieving themselves whenever and wherever they happened to be.

After getting them to go to the outhouse I found I had another problem. They stood on the seats and squatted down instead of sitting on them You could always tell which way they were facing (ha!). As a result, I had to send the cooks to the outhouse every morning with soap and boiling water to wash down the seats. They missed the hole too often and hit the seat.

Another problem I encountered was that the Indians are very private people, and they would not share the outhouse with anyone else. As a result a "four-holer" was useless. I should have built four separate outhouses with one hole each. I also should have built one for my own private use.

During the time I was at the lake, I found hygiene to be of secondary importance because of the severe weather. I never took a bath while I was at the lake. No one did! I tried it once. It was a beautiful sunny day, and I thought I would go to a small stream to bathe. The water was so clear, and it looked so inviting. I took off my clothes and stepped into the water about up to my knees. I could not stand the freezing water. It was so cold that I put on my socks and stepped in again, but I just could not take the freezing water. I put my clothes back on and determined to live like the rest of the workers. I actually found that when living with people who don't bathe, you are better off not to bathe. After a while you cease to notice the smell. Besides that, when you go deer hunting and deer smell you, they just think you are another animal.

I also grew a beard because of the inconvenience of shaving. The constant smoke from burning wet wood and kerosene permeating my clothing made me less than desirable, but I never noticed the smell. It was a smell to which I grew accustomed. I jokingly said to Dr. Jones (co-founder of HCJB), "When I get on the bus to go home, I smell so bad that even the Indians move away from me!" He was amused at that, but there was probably some truth to that statement. Monnie made me strip in the alcove of the front door when I came home. My clothes remained outside until she could wash them.

I needed warm clothing for working in the cold mountain air, so I had another missionary bring me a goose-down coat from the States. I also ordered some thermal underwear and heavy boot socks. I always wore the down coat with the hood as I worked. It became like a uniform to me. I had a complete rain suit, pants and all. It was one of those yellow jobs. I also wore some rubber boots with leather uppers. I purchased rain gear for all of the men who worked for me. They were coats made of solid rubber and very heavy. They couldn't wear their usual ponchos because they got twisted up in them as they worked. As the Indians worked in their rubber coats, they sweat a lot because there were no breathing holes in the rubber. In spite of that, they loved those coats.

I soon realized that horses were vital to getting around in the mountains where there are no roads. I was able to purchase a large strong Arabian horse for my personal transportation. Good mountain horses were hard to find. A horse from the coast cannot function in the mountains because of the lack of oxygen, nor are they strong enough for the muddy trails. I was told by the Indians (who always knew everything that was happening) that a man who lived back in the mountains about nine hours from where we were building the dam needed to sell his horse. I went to look at it, and we agreed on a price. One of my workers rode it back to the dam site. I purchased a new saddle and bridle. Now I was ready to hit the trail!

Don With His Horse, "Flame"

A trail had to be prepared from the road all the way to the lake. It took six hours to walk into the lake so there was a lot of work to be done. Some parts of the trail were worse than others. The marshland and bogs had to be fixed first. Every day, Segundo sent a few men from the camp early in the morning to work on the trail. They took food for two days and cooked and slept wherever they happened to be working, making a lean-to in which to sleep. The men went to a wooded area and cut down trees, dragged them to the marsh and made what was practically a bridge across the marshlands and bogs.

Long poles were cut and laid end to end. Another row of poles was laid parallel to the first row about two and a half feet apart. Then small poles were laid crossways on top of the long poles. On top of the small poles, they put paramo grass. This gave the horses and mules a good trail on which to walk. Bridges across small streams were built in the same manner.

There was no way the horses could go straight down the side of the mountain. It was so steep, they simply would have fallen off the trail. Trails had to be cut out down the sides of the mountains in a zig- zag pattern like switchbacks on a mountain road. Paramo grass was placed on the freshly dug trail so it didn't turn to mud as the horses walked on it. Even with all this work on the trail, we lost five mules during the building of the dam. They rolled down the side of a mountain or fell over a cliff and were killed.

The outboard motor often broke down, and I had to repair it. Without the motor, it would have been nearly impossible to get the supplies across the lake. The chainsaw was temperamental and I had to repair it constantly. The saw was used daily to cut fire wood for cooking. This equipment was vital to the smooth running of the camp. I became very good at repairing things about which I knew nothing beforehand.

During the first phase of the project, I learned a lot about what was involved in feeding a large group of men, such as how many cooks were needed to prepare the food and how much food was needed and how to get it all in to the lake. We ate mostly eggs, beef, rice and cabbage. We also had fresh corn when it was in season. We had a lot of nationally-processed cheese. Soup was prepared for every meal except breakfast. I do not care for soup so the cooks prepared other things for me.

We all ate in the large hut built to serve as the kitchen and dining room. The men ate at tables made of plywood which had been hand carried into the site. They sat on wooden benches which had also been carried in by hand. I always ate by the fire where the cooking was done. Sometimes the smoke was so bad I could hardly breathe, but it was warmer by the fire and it seemed like I was always cold. The Indians, on the other hand, had been born and raised in the high mountains and they were used to these cold conditions. Wood for the fire was cut daily from live stubby trees. The wood never got a chance to dry out so the cooks had a hard time getting it to burn, and as a result, we had a lot of smoke.

We had some wonderful times hunting and fishing. The fishing was so good that I actually got tired of catching rainbow trout. One morning, I was out in the boat and the fish were really biting. I told myself, "After I cast three times and don't get a fish, I will go back to camp." I kept catching fish, so I finally promised myself that I would catch three more trout and go back to camp. When I got back to the campsite, the Indians counted the fish. There were over two hundred rainbow trout! Each one was twelve to fourteen inches in length. I caught some that were twenty-six inches long early in the project. No one but Indians ever fished the lake and even they did not fish there very often. Even though I don't care to eat fish, I love catching them. I gave all the fish to the Indians and they dried them in the kitchen to take home to their families.

Every night and weekends the Indians fished the lake. They used a branch from a tree as a fishing rod. They used only worms on their hooks, but they still caught their fair share and loved it.

Hunting deer in the mountains is hard work. It seemed like we were always going up hill. When we went down that part was quickly over, but the going up was very slow, at least for me. I remember the first shot I ever got at a deer. Segundo and I left camp about four o'clock in the afternoon and walked what seemed to be straight up the mountain for an hour and a half when we spotted three deer in a valley below us. Segundo told me to go down, and he would guide me with hand signals. I made my way down the side of the mountain watching his signals as I went. Finally, I saw the deer below me. I slid down the mountain on my back until I thought I was close enough to shoot. I had heard of hunters getting buck fever and missing their shot, so I took my time and put my sight on the largest deer. I took a deep breath and said to myself, "It's now or never."

The first shot rang out, and the deer dropped in his tracks. The other deer ran, but to my surprise, they came running right back because they didn't know where the shot had come from. I was lying in deep grass and they didn't see me. One of them stopped for just a moment, and I took my second shot. The second deer dropped. The other one kept running, but was confused and when he finally stopped for a moment, I shot him, too! I was so excited, I could hardly contain myself.

Segundo came running down the mountain. Then I asked, "What do we do with three deer to carry back to the site?" He thought I had missed the deer since he heard three shots. He said, "I will drag two deer and you drag the other." We started yelling for the men at the camp to come and pick us up. We finally got the deer to the lake and one of the men came in the boat to take us back to camp. That was a great experience for me, and it gave us meat for the men to eat. Segundo said he had never seen anyone get three deer at the same time and to think that this happened to me, made me very happy. The Indians cut the head off the largest buck and I sent it in to Monnie to have it stuffed and mounted. The taxidermist charged us only $12 at that time.

After we put the trail in a little better shape and my little house was built, and the running water was installed, I thought it was time to have two of my children come to visit me. Our oldest son, Rex, and our oldest daughter, Shari, drove our Land Rover to

Penas Blancas and came in with the muleskinners. It was quite an experience for them. I had no fears for them because I knew the muleskinners would take good care of them. They had a great time and still talk about it to this day. Shari fell in love with my horse, Flame, and we were able to keep him even after the project was finished ... until she left for college. The day after Christmas, I took all four of our children in to the lake. Karlene and Tod, our two youngest children, were no larger than a minute, and it looked so funny to see them mounted on those big horses. As I think back on it now, and see my grandchildren who are the same age, I would never consider letting them take such a dangerous trip, but our children had a ball. However, I think they were very happy to get back to their mother, a warm house and good food.

When I left to work on the project I could hardly speak Spanish even though I had studied Spanish in Costa Rica for a year. Monnie could speak Spanish very well, but it came hard to me. Now I had to run this whole operation with Spanish-speaking Indians. Quichua was their first language and their Spanish was very poor, so I learned to speak Spanish just like they spoke it. This worked out to my advantage later when I had opportunity to preach to the Quichua Indians. They thought I spoke perfect Spanish and they really didn't like to listen when Spanish was really spoken correctly.

By the middle of January, we had the camp in pretty good shape. The work on the trail would never be finished. Rains washed out bridges, and the horses tore up the trail. Landslides covered up some of the trail that had been cut out of the side of the mountains. The trail had to be continually repaired during the whole project.

The men digging the test holes found no clay at all, but God had other plans. He had formed a solid, "U"-shaped rock at the lower end of the lake where the river leaves the lake. It was in the exact spot where we planned to build the earth-filled dam. The men discovered it while looking for clay. The rock was covered with three or four feet of thick mud and muck. I passed this information on to the engineers and suggested we could build a concrete dam.

The engineers mulled this over and came up with all kinds of problems. Since it rained all the time, we couldn't get dry cement into the lake site. It would take thousands of bags of cement and getting it to the lake would be a problem. There was no way to get a concrete mixer in to the site. Blasting would have to be done and no one on the project knew anything about dynamite. Where could we find sand? They decided the job was too massive to try to do by hand.

I had seen firsthand what these Indians could do, however. I knew we *could* get the cement in to the site and keep it dry in plastic bags. All we had to do was to get the equipment to the top of the mountain and the Indians would figure out a way to get it down to the lake. After all, they had been doing this sort of thing all their lives. We could hire more men with mules and carry everything else in to the lake with no problem, and we had found sand at the other end of the lake while looking for clay.

When I presented this to the engineers they said, "We won't be able to find enough workers." I assured them that it would be no problem to get workers. It seemed that everyone wanted to work for us because we fed the men well and the wages were good, and besides that, they always got paid on time. Still the engineers were reluctant to sanction the idea.

Dr. Abe VanDerPuy, president of HCJB World Radio at that time, said, "We must have that dam because we must have the water for the hydro-electric plant." So the engineers agreed to go along with the plan. I felt that it was God's will that the dam should be built, and Monnie and I felt it was God's will for me to continue on the project to see it finished.

Now that a concrete dam was to be built, we had to change our thinking. We had to stockpile enough sand for the dam. The sand had to be dug from the bottom of the lake and taken to the other side of the lake to be washed. The sand was located under about 18 inches of water. I remembered the barges I had seen on the Mississippi river while going to Bible school in St. Louis. I knew that we needed a barge to transport the sand across the lake, so I designed a barge out of twelve fifty-gallon steel drums. The engineers in Pifo welded angle iron on them so they could all be bolted together. These were brought in by mule. Planks, two inches by twelve inches by twelve feet long, were hand carried in to the lake. These were placed on top of the barrels to make a platform, and all bolted together. I connected the barge to the boat with guy wires so it could be pushed back and forth across the lake.

I ordered some hightop rubber boots from the States for the men who would be working in the ice cold water to extract the sand. The sand was shoveled out of the lake onto the barge and pushed across the lake by the motorboat. On the other side, it was shoveled off the barge, placed in wheelbarrows and taken to be washed. A large metal washing tank with holes around the top allowed the water to escape. A gasoline-powered water pump was used to wash the sand. The sand was washed until it was deemed to be clean enough . The test to determine if the sand was clean enough was simple. About an inch of sand was put in a pint jar, filled with water and shaken. When the sand all settled at the bottom and there was less than an eighth inch of silt on top of the sand, it was deemed clean enough. This was important, because, if it was not clean enough, the cement would not adhere to the sand. This would cause a weak dam. The sand was then taken out of the tank and stockpiled near the dam site. By the end of February, we had accumulated about twenty-two cubic yards of sand.

By the first of March, the weather was becoming increasingly cold, wet and windy. We even had some snow. The Indians were having trouble working in that kind of weather. The way the

Indians can tell it is too cold to work is when they can't close their fingers around the handle of a shovel. They wore gloves only when they were working with rock. So in early March, we closed the camp for the rainy season. We took the barge apart, dismantled the water system and put everything in my cabin. Anything that could be carried off by thieves was also stored there. My cabin was closed and a padlock placed on the door. All the Indians in that area knew we were returning so no one bothered the house or tried to break into it.

The Indians all returned to their villages and asked me to let them know when we went to work again. I returned to my job as Director of the Printing Department at HCJB. I had to start planning for the next phase of the project which would be the actual construction of the dam.

Don After a Good Day of Fishing

Chapter 4

God Guides a Moving Vessel

Construction of a concrete dam meant totally different planning than that for an earth-filled dam. For one thing, I had to plan for a much larger work force. We had to purchase tons of cement and I had to plan a way to get it in to the lake and keep it dry until it was used. I needed a whole crew of cooks. It was my conviction that the men had to be fed well as they were working under very difficult conditions. I insisted that they be fed meat at least once a day.

Since blasting was be done for the spillway through solid rock, we needed to purchase lots of dynamite, and we had to transport the explosives over those dangerous trails. All this purchasing of massive amounts of food, cement, dynamite and other supplies was a full-time job and much too much for Monnie with all her other responsibilities. Ralph Horn was asked to help out on the Quito end. At this time, I was named the site engineer by Roger Stubbe (who had taken over from Fred Woodburn as Director of Engineering) and the Field Director. I was given complete control of what happened at the dam site. Ralph was to do all the purchasing and keep the supply line running. Roberto would continue hauling all the supplies to *Penas Blancas*. I knew we needed more storage space at *Penas Blancas* so I had a small portable house taken to that spot to provide more storage and better security for the supplies. This gave us two small houses at *Penas Blancas*.

Segundo Bustamante, my foreman on the job during the first phase, agreed to work with me during the second phase. Segundo and his wife hired all the men we needed from the mountain region. All they had to do was let it be known we were going to hire and they had more men wanting the job than we could use. We paid the men one dollar a day, three good meals a day and a place to sleep. The Indians considered that a good deal. Segundo found a man who had ten mules and hired him and his mules to haul all the supplies to the lake.

On September 8, 1970, Roberto and I left Quito for *Penas Blancas*. We were joined there by the first twenty men we hired and the ten mules. My horse was also brought out to *Penas Blancas*. The mules were all loaded and we were ready to leave for the lake. When a mule is being loaded he is blind-folded. When he is blindfolded, he is very peaceful and a person can walk all around him without having to be careful. Otherwise, they kick like crazy and are very dangerous.

We hired only twenty men for the first week to re-open the camp and start repairing the trail. This number increased almost weekly until at the peak of the building, we had 120 men working. We also had twenty mules making a round trip each day except on Sunday. Every man carried a load into the lake each time he entered. They carried in things the mules could not carry such as lumber too long to go on the side of a mule and many other items. This way, we managed to get all the supplies to the lake.

We sent the boat to the lake first because it had to be there in order to take the men and supplies across the lake. The boat had been brought out after the first phase. It would have been too great a temptation for thieves if it had been stored in the little house.

Going to the lake in September was a mistake on my part. It was the end of the rainy season and very cold. The wind was blowing a gale and the rain turned to sleet and made the trip miserable. The trail was in terrible condition. Several of the mules got stuck in the mud and had to be unloaded and pulled out. The horse carrying the outboard motor fell and rolled down the mountain. Thankfully, he was not hurt and the motor was not damaged.

The first few days, the men spent all their time cleaning and repairing the thatch-roofed buildings and working on the trail. My little cabin was white from mildew and had to be cleaned from top to bottom. The barge had to be reassembled and the water system set up. The first few days were really difficult. The temperature dropped to twenty degrees at night and reached no higher than fifty-eight degrees during the day. It was a wet cold that seemed almost unbearable as it penetrated to the bone.

Cooks Busy at Work

We hired five cooks to prepare all the food. One cook brought his wife as one of the cooks and she was the only female on the job for the entire time. This couple slept in the kitchen where all the food was stored. At first, we brought fresh butchered beef on the side of a mule for the men to eat. Then one day I said to myself,

"That is dumb! That cow can walk in by itself." So from then on, we brought in a steer every two weeks. It was walked to the lake and taken across the lake on the barge. The Indians killed it and butchered it. I was present when the first steer was killed. To my surprise, when the throat was cut on the steer, the Indians started sucking the blood from the wound. Their faces were covered with blood and they were laughing and jumping around. It really was a gruesome sight. I promptly had a meeting with all the men and told them that the Bible forbids the drinking of blood and since this was a Christian organization, we would not permit the drinking of blood. I read to them, from the Bible, where we were commanded not to drink blood. Even though they were not believers, they all respected the Bible and we never had that problem again. However, you could almost tell each time a steer was killed that they were thinking, "What a waste of good blood."

Indians Butchering Cow

The Indians eat every part of the steer. They ate everything that is found in the head—you can use your imagination as to what I mean. They always cut out the loin for me. They cut the hide into a large circle, then starting from the outside, they cut in a circular pattern until the hide was one long strip about one-inch wide. The strip was taken outside, twisted very tightly and strung up between two posts to dry. This gave the men rawhide rope which is very strong. It was a help in carrying supplies to the lake. There was literally no part of the steer that went unused.

The men all worked in two-week shifts. We split the work force into two groups. The first group worked two weeks and then had four days off. They walked out to the road where they were met by trucks. After they received their pay, they were taken home. Four days later, they returned for two more weeks of work. The second group followed the same schedule. That gave us workers at all times at the site. We worked every day except Sunday. Every two weeks, Segundo went home like the others, and during that time he purchased the steer to be brought to the lake to be slaughtered.

We needed a dock for the boat and barge so we built one out of timber we found near the lake. The dock was covered with paramo grass and served the purpose very nicely.

With all the activity going on and because of the large amount of supplies we needed, a communication system became absolutely necessary. We took a two-way radio to the lake, and a portable power plant was brought in. The portable plant was old and proved to be another frustration to me. It always took at least an hour to get it started. I had a daily contact with Monnie at four o'clock in the afternoon, so I had the men start trying to start the plant no later than three o'clock. This radio contact was our only link to the outside. It was like a breath of fresh air to talk to Monnie each day. I always had a list of things I needed. She passed that list on to Ralph and he purchased what was needed.

Sometimes Monnie wanted me to talk to one of the children, so I would have to straighten them out over the radio. It was kind of hard to tell them something and say, "Over." Then they said, "Yes, sir - over," but it all worked out just fine. That's what you call ruling from a distance. Monnie called it *distance disciplining.*

In the men's dorm, we built a platform on each side where they placed their straw mats and blankets. This kept the men from having to sleep on the ground. It also gave them a place under their bunk to store personal things. I purchased a straw mat for each man. They provided their own bedding which usually consisted of their poncho and maybe one blanket. They slept in their clothes and in pairs to keep each other warm against the relentless cold.

An Overview of the Campsite at Lake Loreto

Back at the lake, we had to clean all the mud and muck off the U-shaped rock and it was obvious that the muck had to go somewhere! What wasn't so obvious was where to put it. We started throwing it in to the river but the river soon clogged up because the current was not fast enough to wash it downstream. So, we finally decided to throw it over on the other side of the mountain. However, when the mountain towers 100 feet over your head, it is no simple matter to just throw it over. We cut platforms in the hillside about four feet apart, up the side of the mountain. Then, we stationed a man with a shovel on each platform. One man dug a shovelful of muck from the riverbed and threw it up to the platform above him. Then, the man on that platform took that same shovelful of muck and threw it up the platform above him, and so on, up and over the mountaintop to slide down the other side. This was no small job as there was four to five feet of muck on the rock and it took at least 25 platforms to reach the top of that 100-foot crest.

It was about 200 yards from the camp to the dam site. The trail got so muddy and slushy that it was hard for the men to get to work so we built a walkway. Lots of logs about two or three feet long were cut and placed along the trail. Boards were carried in and placed on top of the logs. Now, we had a sturdy boardwalk all the way to where the men were working.

Segundo told me that we must fire one or two men every week so that the rest of the men would know that we meant business. I left this job up to Segundo as he knew which ones were the least productive workers. Segundo was a hard taskmaster, but the workers respected him.

One day, I was watching a worker who was goofing off and not getting any work done. I watched him for about fifteen minutes and finally walked over to where he was standing and said, "I've been watching you for at least fifteen minutes. Don't you want to work?" He told me he **did** want to work. I said, "I've been watching you and you haven't been working, so I don't think you really want to work here. I'm going to give you one more chance and if I ever catch you not working, again, you are done. You can just pick up your pay and leave." This worker turned out to be one of my best workers.

After the muck was taken off the U-shaped rock and the rock was washed down with a high pressure hose, it was time for the engineers to make the final plans for the dam. Two HCJB engineers, Herb Jacobson (a genius at all things involving engineering) and Gordon Wolfram (a civil engineer) came into the site. They spent four days at the lake, drawing up the actual plans for the dam. When they were completed they turned them over to me and said, "This is what you do!" The engineers never came back to the lake after that. They either had faith in me or they didn't like the weather.

Without a doubt, the biggest job we had to do was to blast a channel through solid rock. This channel had to be more than 200 yards long, two yards wide and two yards deep. None of us had ever worked with dynamite before, but we found there is not much to it. You just drill a hole, put in some dynamite, light the fuse and run (ha)! Well ..., there is a little more to it than that.

A man who worked at the hydroelectric plant at Papallacta had some experience with dynamite, so he was brought up to the site for a week to teach us some of the basics. He showed us how to put the caps in the dynamite and what we should do to keep from getting blown up. The caps were hand carried in by the muleskinners so they would not be in close proximity to the dynamite in case a mule went over the side of the mountain. The cap is the most critical part of the dynamite. A person can have his hand blown off very easily if great care is not taken. A hole is cut in the stick of dynamite and the cap is placed into it and sealed. Everything, even the dynamite itself, had to be put in plastic bags because everything was so wet. The rain even filled the holes that were drilled in the rock.

We started the blasting procedure by drilling holes in the rock with a sledge hammer and bit, but that was so slow that we realized we needed a power drill and jackhammer. That meant we had to have an air compressor.

A compressor cost about $10,000, and that was not in the budget, but it had to be purchased. After permission was granted to purchase the compressor, we had to figure out a way to get it to the lake. It was simply impossible to bring a compressor in by mule or by hand.

Helicopter Bringing in the Air Compressor

Fortunately, the Texaco Oil Company was building a pipeline across the mountains and flew many helicopters in the area taking supplies to their crews. They agreed to bring the compressor in, but since we were nearly 14,000 feet up in the mountains, they had to wait until the atmospheric conditions were just right. On a sunny day there was not enough air to keep the helicopter aloft. A rainy day was good, but when it rained there was almost always fog. We waited three days for the weather to be just right.

The pilot told me,"Okay, we will try it, but if we start going down, I will cut the compressor loose and let it fall." Thank the Lord, we made it. It was a little disgusting, though. It took us only about three minutes to get to the lake from the hydroelectric plant. On foot it takes nearly six hours. Wouldn't it have been nice to have had our own helicopter? This was the only piece of equipment brought in that way. Everything else was brought in by mule or by hand.

We brought in one hundred pound sacks of fertilizer (nitro) to be used with the dynamite. The fertilizer by itself is harmless, but in a hole with dynamite, it is equal to dynamite in its power to break up rock. The fertilizer was much cheaper than dynamite. We packed it in plastic bags which were the same circumference as the dynamite and we made them the same length. We had men filling these bags every day.

The dynamite had to be stored in a dry place far from the camp, so we built a small thatch-roofed house and put it on stilts about four feet off the ground. This house was about three hundred yards from the camp. A padlock was placed on the door and Segundo and I had the only keys. The caps had to be kept dry, also. Since the cap and fuse could tolerate little or no dampness, we kept them in the kitchen where the humidity was lower. The caps were stored above the open fire hanging from the thatched roof. The cooks were not very happy about this arrangement.

We had to stockpile ahead of time, the dynamite caps and little bags of fertilizer that we needed once we started blasting. All the time, the trail was being worked on and sand was brought across the lake and stockpiled. We had to meet the mules who brought the supplies each day and boat the supplies across the lake. This took lots of planning and organization. Segundo and I got together daily to plan the next day's work and to decide how to split up the men and their work.

Now that we had the compressor, we needed gasoline to run it. We purchased six, fifteen-gallon barrels and filled each of them with ten gallons of gas. A mule could not carry fifteen gallons of gas on each side—it was just too heavy for him. However, we found another problem. Ten gallons did not fill up the barrels and the gas sloshed around, making it hard for the mule to keep his balance going up and down the mountains. The muleskinners had to be very careful with these mules.

The danger of one of the workers getting blown up or someone getting seriously injured or ill was always a possibility so Dr. Wally Swanson, a missionary doctor at our Quito hospital, gave me written instructions on how to handle many different scenarios. He also sent me medication for all kinds of sickness or injuries, including morphine in the case of a very serious mishap. That made me the official doctor on the site! I had never given an injection in my entire life. However, we only had some minor problems (thank the Lord), and nothing life-threatening happened. In fact, during the entire project, we never had to send a man home because of sickness or accident. That, in itself, is a miracle considering the primitive conditions, the severe weather and the difficult problems we faced.

On one occasion, we might have lost a lot of men. Segundo was bringing a group of men from the other end of the lake on the barge. As they approached the dock, all the men went to one side of the barge, ready to get off. The barge capsized and all the men went into the water. Only a few of them could swim. We still aren't sure how they all got out of the water. We believed it to be the Lord's hand of protection.

When we started the blasting, we saw that some of the rocks would fly all the way to the camp. I didn't want any rocks going through the tin roof of my cabin, so I had the men put a heavy thatched roof over the tin. That way the rocks did not make holes in my roof.

My four children made several trips to the lake to visit me. These proved to be memorable times in their lives. I remember once when Rex brought in a friend. They challenged each other to dive off the barge into the icy cold water and swim to shore. One day, they both went to the barge and I thought they would "chicken out", but to my surprise, they dove into the lake. They almost froze, but after putting on dry clothes and drinking a cup of hot chocolate, they were fine again.

Another fond memory is the evening we all went to the lakeside and threw empty catsup bottles into the lake with many of the workers watching. I took my 357 Blackhawk revolver and we started shooting at the bottles. I let some of the workers, as well as the children, take aim at the bottles. Some of us came close, but Shari popped bottle after bottle. I turned to the workers and jokingly said, "Don't ever mess with my daughter."

One night, Tod got sick and vomited all over the floor. It has always been Monnie's job to clean up that kind of a mess. I could not stand the smell and every time I attempted to clean it up, I gagged and nearly lost it, too. The other children made no attempt to help me so I got a bottle of Pinesol I had for cleaning the cabin and poured the whole bottle on the floor. I finally got it all cleaned up. Oh, how I missed my good wife, Monnie!

Karlene remembers the cookies I made at the camp. It was a secret recipe from my mother. I came from a poor family that went through the Great Depression. This recipe was about the best we could do during those days. I will share it with you: Take powdered sugar and put in a little milk and a drop of vanilla. Stir it until it makes a thick frosting. Take two graham crackers, put the frosting between them and it makes a delicious cookie! Karlene loved them. The children also thought it was fun to sit around the fire and eat. They loved the fried meat and potatoes the cooks prepared for them.

With the compressor in place, it was possible to drill holes in the solid rock more quickly, and we were ready to begin blasting the channel. One or two bags of nitro were dropped into the bottom of the drilled hole and the dynamite was dropped in on top of that. A little dirt was put in on top of the explosives and then it was packed down so the blast would not just blow straight back up the hole. The fuses extended out of the holes about two-and-a-half feet and four feet into the hole.

Once all the explosives were set in the holes, and men were ready to light the fuses, all the workers were removed from the area. Two or three workers ran to the kitchen and each man got a red-hot stick. With the red-hot stick in hand, they ran from one stick of dynamite to the next, lighting the fuses. They had to blow on the stick to get it hot enough to light the fuses. Then, they fled the area until the dynamite went off.

Sometimes there was a stick of dynamite that did not go off. When one didn't immediately go off, no one was allowed into the area for five to ten minutes, as it could possibly eventually go off. I never let the men take any chances. All the men were kept well back until we were absolutely sure that it was not going to go off and even then, it was very nerve-racking to go in and replace the charge.

When a charge did not go off, it had to be redone. To remove the charges, we devised a little recovery tool. We attached a tiny spoon to the end of a long narrow rod. This was used to scoop all the dirt from the hole and get the dynamite out. Then we put in another charge and tried again.

The rocks were cleared from the channel after the blasting. This was done by forming a human chain. A man picked up a rock and tossed it to another man, he in turn threw it to another man, and so on. There were between 40 and 50 men in this human chain. In this way the rocks were cleared from the area. They were stacked out of the way about fifty yards from the channel.

At the same time, we had a group of rockcutters cutting blocks of rock 32 by 16 by 16 inches. These men were blasting out the side of another mountain about one mile from the site. The rocks were handcut with chisels and the men carried the blocks to the dam site. Each block weighed about 80 pounds. We stockpiled 10,000 of these blocks to be placed in the pouring of the concrete for the dam.

Removing Rock from the Channel

While we were stockpiling the sand and the rocks, we were also cutting the channel. At that time, we realized we had no gravel to mix with the sand and cement, so we put a group of the men on the large rockpile that had been taken out of the channel. These men separated the small rocks that could be used for gravel. It soon became obvious that they were not getting enough of the gravel-size rock, so I bought 30 small sledge hammers and put 30 men to work breaking up the bigger rocks into tiny rocks for the gravel. This was also stockpiled near the sand and the cut blocks.

We finally finished enough of the channel to begin working on the gates that were to control the water leaving the lake. A reinforced concrete beam was made across the top of the channel with grooves in it for the gates to go up and down. These gates went all the way to the bottom of the channel. We could keep all the water in the lake or release some of it as it was needed at the hydroelectric plant below. The water ran down the mountain in the existing river to the plant below. It takes one hour for the water to reach the plant from the dam. The three gates were all set in concrete while the rest of the channel was blasted out. All the time, I had a man with a jackhammer squaring up the sides and smoothing out the bottom of the channel.

The worksite was a beehive of activity—every man with a simple job to do, but every job essential for the project we had undertaken. I never stopped to wonder if we were foolish to take on such a challenge. This dam was needed for the work of the Lord—He would make it happen.

Bringing Supplies Across the Lake

Chapter Five

Final Stages

Up to this point, the water coming out of the lake was still flowing down the old riverbed. We now needed to divert the river to flow through the gates and down the new channel we had just blasted out. We dug another channel from the lake about 200 yards out to meet the existing path of the river. We then made a make-shift dam out of dirt, rocks and stumps at the existing outlet of the river forcing the water to follow the new path we had made for it.

Once the water was running down the new temporary riverbed, we were able to dig another channel from the gates all the way to the lake and right up to the makeshift dam. This channel was dug through nothing but mud. It had to be six feet wide and six feet deep, just like the rock channel to which it was connected. The idea was to later cut a small channel across and join these two channels and have the water flow down the new channel we had cut through solid rock. This would enable us to clean off the rest of the U-shaped rock where the dam was to be constructed.

It was during this time back in Quito that some Spanish workers were complaining to the engineers that they had no jobs because I hired only Indians. The engineers told me I had to hire these Spanish workers, so I told them to come on out. About 20 of them came out on a Tuesday. They arrived about two o'clock in the afternoon and we put them to work in the mud. They had never seen anything like this before and when we got up the next morning, they had all gone home. An Indian told me they left about three o'clock that morning for Quito. We never had that problem again!

We made that small channel and the water did just what we wanted it to do and we started cleaning up the entire U-shaped rock. A high pressure hose was used to clean the remaining mud off the rock. Now after many months, we were ready to start on the dam itself.

We were ready for the keying of the dam. We cut straight down into the U-shaped rock, making beveled holes. The purpose of the bevel was so that as the pressure of the water built up against the dam, the dam would push down against the solid rock and so it would not tip over. We also cut square holes 20 by 20 by 20 inches. These were cut so the dam would not slide off its foundation. They acted like keys in a keyhole and this gave the dam stability and kept it from sliding or tilting. We keyed the dam in twelve places. The engineers were very accurate in their calculations. In 1985, there was a devastating earthquake very near the dam which tore up the jungle area just below the power plant and hundreds, if not thousands of people were killed. Small villages were totally destroyed. The dam held perfectly. It was quite an engineering feat.

The dam was not all that big, but the way it had to be built made it a big job. Once on my way to Quito, I spent the night at the road and talked to some of the men with Texaco who were building the pipeline across the Andes. I said, "I can't believe what you are doing with these big D-8 cats." One of the men said, "Well, we can't believe what you are doing by hand. We have every piece of equipment we need to do our job, and we can't believe what you are doing with nothing. We talk about it back at our camp and none of us want your job."

Every time I went to Quito, I had to get lots of supplies for the job and personal things for myself. Monnie washed all my clothes. Everything had to be packed in plastic because of the rain. Breakable items had to be packed in such a way that they would not be broken. I had to plan as if my horse were going to roll down the mountain and I didn't want anything to get broken. Many times, I had to jump off my horse as he lost his footing and went over the side of the mountain. Fortunately, he was never seriously hurt (but I was not always so fortunate).

We did have some exciting times, though. One night, one of the men saw a mountain lion up by the outhouse. They came running to tell me. I got my rifle, tucked my 357 revolver in my belt and started up the hill. When we started up the hill, there were several Indians behind me with machetes, but as I climbed the steps, fewer followed. As it turned out, the mountain lion had left. We saw several in the mountains, but never got a shot at one.

I had better luck with bear. Three Indians and I left to go deer hunting one weekend. We walked only about three hours when we saw three black forms coming up the valley. The Indians said, "Bears!" I had never seen a bear in the wild in my life. We ran up the mountainside so we could get a shot at them. Now understand, *there are no trees to climb at 14,000 feet* and we were charging at the bears. The Indians said, "Shoot the largest one first." It happened that it was a mother with two half-grown cubs. I shot the mother and one of the cubs. We were all very excited because none of us had ever bagged a bear before.

We carried the bears back to camp to feed the men. I wanted to get the smaller bear stuffed, so I looked through my sporting magazines to show Monnie how I wanted it stuffed. In all the magazines, I found that a mother bear with cubs is extremely dangerous. Since we didn't know this, we had no fear. In this case, ignorance was bliss! I sent the large hide home with an Indian to get it cured, but his dogs got hold of it and tore it up. I did get the smaller bear stuffed.

One day, we received orders from our personnel office in Quito to get all the vital information from every worker so they could be covered by the Ecuadorian social security. Segundo and I started filling out papers. Very few of the men knew their ages, so we just guessed. When it came to the date of birth, they were at a total loss. As a result, many of the Indians were born on August 27 which is my birthdate. The rest just happened to be born on Segundo's birthday. The Indians don't really care when they were born. They just know that it must have happened some time in the past.

Bringing the Cement Mixer in by Hand

Now that the keying of the dam was done and a lot of the material was stockpiled, we really needed the cement mixer. It had been sitting at the hydroplant waiting for a good day for a helicopter to bring it into the lake. We could wait no longer, so I had it brought by truck to the top of the mountain. It would have to be carried in by hand. Segundo and I sent 21 men out to the road to bring in the mixer. We sent the men out to the road a day ahead of time and they slept by the road on top of the mountain that night.

Early the next morning, they started back to the lake. There was no way the mixer could be brought across the lake on the barge so they had to hand carry it into the lake the long way—over Heartbreak Ridge.

The mixer was tied between two long poles and most of the men were used to carry the bulk of the weight. However, going up a mountain, the men needed help so they tied ropes on the top of the mixer and some of the men pulled. Going down, the ropes were used as a brake. Other long poles were cut to help steady the mixer when it tilted from one side to the other. The trail was muddy and slick and not wide enough for the men to walk two abreast. There were always some of the men who were off the trail trying to keep their balance. In some places, the mixer had to be dragged and in other places, they let it slide down the mountain. They were slipping and sliding for twelve long hours, but they made it even though it rained most of the time.

Hundreds of planks, 12 feet long, 12 inches wide and one inch thick were hand carried into the lake. The planks were cut from green logs and were very heavy. It made it very difficult to carry them across the mountains because they were so heavy. The planks were used to erect forms in which the cement would be poured to form the dam.

Segundo had the men make six little boxes, 18 inches wide, 18 inches long and 12 inches deep. They nailed a long pole on each side so two men could carry the box, one on each end. These boxes were all the same size so we could get our cement mixture right. There were six men who brought three boxes of sand, four men who brought two boxes of gravel and two men who brought one box of cement while others carried buckets of water from the river. All this was thrown into the cement mixer and mixed. We had men that ran the mixer to determine when it was mixed enough.

While the cement was being mixed, the men ran back and got their boxes filled again. The men always ran back and forth as this is the way they worked all their lives. When the concrete was mixed, it was dumped into a wheelbarrow, taken to the dam and poured into the forms. Some of the planks were laid on top of the freshly-dumped cement so the wheelbarrows didn't sink down into the concrete. This gave the men something solid to walk on. We had another crew of men working on the forms all the time.

The forms had to be in place before the cement was dumped. They had to go up as the dam grew higher. Every night when we stopped for the day, some jagged rocks were placed in the freshly poured concrete so that they stuck up above the level of the concrete. The next day when the new concrete was poured, it clung to the tops of the jagged rocks. This was the procedure we followed every day. We were fortunate in that it rained all the time and the concrete never really set up overnight during the entire pouring. It was always still damp every morning when we went to work and we poured the new concrete on top of the concrete poured the day before. As it slowly dried, it became one big solid slab of concrete, completely fused. There was no other reinforcement in the dam except for the 10,000 handcut rocks, some of which were placed in the concrete each day as we poured the wet cement.

We built a wooden form on the backside of the dam so that the back would go straight up. The form looked like a long, high wall. On the front side, we stepped it. The base was about 22 feet wide and it stepped up to the top which was only two feet wide. As we filled each step with concrete, we used a vibrator to force out pockets of air and force concrete into all the little nooks, crannies and corners. Using a vibrator was an important job and it had to be done right. If the vibrator is run too long, the gravel and sand will separate from the concrete. We had one man who loved this job and he was very good at it.

The construction site was a flurry of activity. Men were running everywhere. Each knew his job and performed it perfectly. Some mixed cement, others carried gravel, some carried cement, others carried water, some carried eighty-pound rocks to be placed in the fresh cement while still others were running wheelbarrows, dumping cement and running back to the mixer for another load. Then our friend was there with the vibrator and others were building the forms and some were bringing bags of cement to the site from the storage hut. All this was being done under very hazardous and uncomfortable conditions.

All this time the mules were bringing in hundred pound bags of cement and all our food over the muddy trails. We still had men working on the trail every day. The mules tore up parts of the trail daily as they came in with their heavy loads.

The Dam Under Construction

Segundo and the men knew how many bags of cement they could mix each day. We realized the supply of cement we had on hand and the bags of cement the mules were bringing in each day would not be enough to meet the amount we needed daily. I talked to the men and they said, "Let's hand carry in enough to finish the job." To me, that seemed impossible, but we needed the cement. I suggested splitting the bags, putting fifty pounds in plastic bags and carrying it in that way. The men told me it would be easier to carry the full bag of one hundred pounds. They suggested we send out two men for each bag of cement and that they trade off on the way in. So we sent men out early each morning and they returned that evening with the cement. This was *in addition* to the daily loads the mules were bringing in.

The pouring of the dam was finally completed and we started removing the forms. We had other men (cement finishers) put the final touches on the dam. The rails for the three gates were put in place and the final work on the gates was finished. The entire dam area was washed with a high pressure hose.

Don On the Completed Dam

On the front side of the dam where anyone in the area could read it, we inscribed the words, *"Agua para la gloria de Dios,"* which translates, "Water for the glory of God." The Scripture reference, Revelation 22:18 was also inscribed.

We knew there would really be very few people who would ever see the inscription, but all the deerhunters and fishermen who came through the area would see it. On the very top of the dam, we had an engraved plaque with the words in Spanish, "Constructed by Donald Schroder and Segundo Bustamante and 100 valiant men."

Now it was time to open the new channel that was dug through the mud right up to the temporary dam. We had to remove the temporary dam so the water could run freely down the freshly cut channel. We decided the best way to remove the temporary dam was to blast it out. We took all the explosives we had left and placed them in the temporary dam. A large charge of dynamite and fifteen hundred pounds of nitro was carefully placed in the earth-filled dam.

I had all four of our children come out to the lake for the big blast. After all the explosives were set in place and the "big bang" was about the happen, we made sure all the men were far, far away. We had never set off this much explosive at one time before. The children and I went high up the side of the mountain above my cabin to watch the blast. We had a very long fuse on the explosives so the man who lit it could get away.

After we were sure all the men were safe, we gave the signal for him to light the fuse. He lit the fuse and ran like crazy. I think he was still running when the blast occurred! The blast was much larger than I had expected. We were at what I thought was a safe distance from the blast, but we got showered by rocks. I threw myself over our youngest children to protect them from the falling rocks. Thank the Lord, none of us was injured. One worker above us did get hit by a flying rock, but it was not serious.

It really was a beautiful sight. Mud, dirt and rocks flying through the air was really something to see. I am glad the children were there to see it. The blast blew the temporary dam completely away, opening up the channel so the water ran freely.

After eleven months of work in the high Andes mountains, under severe weather conditions and primitive living conditions, the Lake Loreto dam was completed. More than 110 tons of supplies and equipment were carried in by mule back and by hand over extremely muddy and treacherous trails. The dam itself stood 22 feet high and stretched some 50 yards across the top. There were no major accidents among the workers, but five mules lost their lives slipping from the trail and plunging down the mountainside.

We started planning for the dedication of the dam. I wanted to have some special food both for the workers and the missionaries who would make the long walk to the lake. Segundo purchased four large pigs. We thought the pigs could walk in the way the steers did, but their feet were much smaller and they just sank into the mud. The men bringing them in wound up carrying them most of the way. The cooks were going to prepare *fritada* (fried pork) for the dedication.

After killing the pigs, their hair was burned off and the hide was stripped off (the heat released the hide from the melted grease beneath it). The meat was then cut into about two-inch pieces and cooked over an open fire in a large, shallow brass pan, similar to a Chinese wok. It was left to cook all day. They seasoned it with lots of salt. It makes a delicious meal. They also had lots of other typical Indian food.

Many missionaries were coming to the dedication, so I sent several Indians out to the road to accompany them to the lake. Our two oldest children, Rex and Shari, also came for the dedication. The Indians carried all the sleeping bags and dry clothing that our guests brought with them.

Dedication Service for the Dam

The dedication of the dam was held at dawn on March 22, 1971. The rest of the day was spent showing people around and eating. We all had a great time. Early the next morning, we sent all the missionaries and Rex and Shari back to the main road. The Indians again guided them and carried out all their belongings.

Now, we had to reverse our thinking and start sending things back to the road. We dismantled all we could and packed it out. The Indians wanted to buy many of the items, so we sold them all the tables and benches. Some even wanted the picks and shovels they had used. We gave them a very good price. The biggest problem we faced was getting a helicopter to take out the compressor. By this time, the workforce was down to just enough men to clean up the area. The helicopter finally made it in and took out the compressor and the cement mixer.

Then, it was time to say goodbye to the dam and the old campsite. As we left the camp, I told some of the Indians I would come and visit them in their villages and homes. Knowing the remote location of their villages and the austerity of the mountains and the weather, they said, "You will never come and visit us," but I promised that I would, anyway. They placed a challenge before me and I love a challenge! I made up my mind right then that, God willing, I would keep my promise to visit them. Again, I had no idea what lay ahead.

Chapter 6

It Isn't Just "Either ... Or"

HCJB needed more water in order to produce more electrical power for our transmitters. The purpose was to be able to send the good news of the Gospel around the world via shortwave radio with a stronger signal. However, we dared not forget the lost souls right around us. If we are to be missionaries for Jesus Christ, *going across the street* is every bit as important and effective as *going across the ocean.* I felt that these workers on the dam, and their families, needed Christ as much as the people in some far-away country whom I would never meet. During the project, the leadership of HCJB agreed with me and gave me full authority to have Bible studies even if it took the men off the job at times.

I started having informal Bible studies every night and teaching the men some Christian choruses. I found that they loved to sing. They were very interested in the Bible studies and started asking a lot of questions. None of these men were Christians; they knew little or nothing about the Bible.

For years, the Gospel Missionary Union and HCJB worked with the Quichua Indians around Colta (further to the south) and some progress was made. It was just so very hard! Many of these people did not even speak the language of their country (Spanish) —they were terribly isolated ... even from their own countrymen. The situation brought about deep suspicion in these Indians toward the rest of the world.

One missionary visited in Colta and was introduced to the wife of one of the Indian leaders. The missionary was not very tall, but the Indian lady was even shorter. As their eyes met, the missionary extended her hand for the traditional South American handshake. Looking into those dark eyes, the missionary despaired of finding a way across the language barrier, the culture barrier and ... suddenly, she realized that her extended hand was not met by a hand, but by a tiny hand *covered with a rough poncho.* It seemed that these women were light years apart—estranged by time and culture, as well as by language. Later, she questioned a fellow missionary as to why the Indian woman had covered her hand. Tears welled up in her eyes as she was told, "The Indian doesn't think she is good enough to touch the skin of a white person." This is the chasm which discrimination and oppression built. Bridging it was no easy matter.

In spite of the chasm that separated us, Segundo Bustamante accepted the Lord when I presented the gospel to him during the very first phase of the project. As I lived and worked with the Indians every day, we learned to know each other as men. The barriers crumbled and a bridge of trust and friendship developed bit by bit much as the dam became a reality one shovelful of cement at a time. The Indians already believed that Christ was born of the Virgin Mary and that He died on the cross and rose again, but they never incorporated those facts into their own lives. They also believed the Bible was the Word of God and inspired.

They all had been baptized into the State church at birth and they were taught to make the Virgin Mary the pillar of their faith. They were also told that Christians did not believe in Mary and they should avoid them—not listen to them. So we began teaching them what the Bible says about the virgin birth. When they saw that our Bible said that Mary was truly a virgin and that we, too, believed she was a virgin at the time of the birth of Christ, they were more willing to listen.

Night after night, the men came to the kitchen around the open fire to sing choruses and study the Bible. I am sure that many of them, at first, came out of boredom—just to have something to do. After all, they were six hours from the road and another two hours by truck to the nearest town, so they were stuck at the site. Besides that, they may have thought that I would fire them if they didn't come and listen to me. Once they learned some choruses, they came gladly. We ordered some little chorus books, with words only, and had them sent out to the site. The men loved the little books even though many of them could not read which (being a proud people) they never wanted known. They opened the chorus books and sang at the top of their lungs, pretending to be reading all the words.

Don Conducting a Bible Study in the Kitchen

After a few weeks, I gave an invitation for anyone who wanted to accept Christ. A first, they couldn't understand what that meant. I explained that it meant they could have a new life in Christ and know they were on their way to heaven. After they understood that their lives could be changed and their sins forgiven, they began to accept Christ, one by one. One hundred and forty three

Indians accepted Christ during the eleven months it took to build the dam.

As these men came to know Christ, I realized they needed some instruction on Christian living. I invited Enoch Sanford from Quito to come back to teach them how to live the Christian life. He came in and spent a week at a time. Every day after lunch he taught them for an hour, and then again for another hour in the evening. Enoch made several trips like this to the lake site. Later on, Carlos Jarrin from HCJB's Evangelism Department came in with Christian films. The little power plant and the projector had to be hand carried in to the lake each time. These films were on the life of Christ. Carlos also made several trips in to the lake site.

Workers Listening to the Bible Lessons

Since the men worked two weeks and had four days off, the only time we had them all at the camp at the same time was on Thursdays. We had our "formal" church service on Thursday night. It was still rather informal with the men sitting under the meat which was hanging from the roof. Some of the men sat on 100-pound bags of rice and others on bags of sugar. The open fire was burning and the only light we had was a Coleman-type lantern hanging at the front of the kitchen shed.

During all those months of digging and blasting, the Lord was at work building His church. These men's lives truly did change, not because I was there teaching them, but because God touched their hearts and changed their lives. I was just there as His servant doing what I could. "Without Him we can do nothing." Thank God for the opportunity we had to share the gospel with these men. Thank God I didn't say, "No" to Him, that "It is too much to ask," or "I can't do it."

Toward the end of the project, the men showed an interest in getting baptized. I knew that the water in the lake was very cold and I wondered how I could stand to be in that cold water long enough to baptize all these men. We set a day for the baptismal service and all the men gathered on the lakeshore.

They gave testimonies and sang songs. I asked Enoch to come back and give a message on the lakeshore. We wanted it to be a serious time when they understood the obedience and symbolism of identification with the death, burial and resurrection of Christ. Then it was time for the baptism. I put on goose-down underwear, goose-down booties, boot socks, my clothes over that, and on top of that I wore a pair of chest waders I borrowed from another missionary. I stepped into the water and it didn't feel bad at all. The men took off their shirts and boots. As they stepped into the water, they let out a startling gasp in spite of themselves. This made the other men laugh. It was not your typical baptismal service.

Baptismal Servince in the Cold Lake Water

I thought I was so smart with all my protection from the icy cold water, but as I baptized each man, my arm went under the water and as I brought the men up out of the water, my arm went up above my shoulder. The water started running down inside the waders. The further down into my waders the water went, the faster I baptized! We prepared hot coffee for the men who were baptized. Just as soon as they came out of the water, they ran to put on dry clothes and get some hot coffee to warm themselves on the inside.

Since we had our main church service on Thursday night so all the men could attend, most of the men who were still in camp went fishing or hunting on Saturday afternoon and Sunday. Many times, I took two or three men hunting with me. They knew the mountains like the back of their hands and could guide me back to camp if I got lost. They also carried the deer I shot back to camp.

Sometimes we went hunting on horseback so we could go deeper into the mountains. These trips took us where there were no trails at all, over mountains as high as 14,000 to 15,000 feet. When we arrived at a place that seemed good for hunting, we set up camp and walked out through the mountains from there. Sometimes the fog rolled in and we couldn't see anything. That's when I felt safe with the Indians. They never got lost.

One day, as we came over a very high ridge, I looked through my binoculars to see if there were any deer in the deep valley. To my surprise I saw what looked like a hut. Then I saw another one. There were several huts down there and I asked the Indians if people lived down there. They told me it was a refuge for fugitives from the law. I said, "We should go down there some day and tell them about the Lord." They became very excited and said, "No!! They will kill you. They shoot at us when we fish the river near there. Do not go down there!"

The Village of Oyacachi

The Indians seemed very nervous and anxious to get out of there even though we were several miles from the village and up on a high ridge. We returned to camp, but I could not get this little village out of my mind.

After the completion of the dam, I returned to my duties as Director of the HCJB Printing Department. My experience working with the Quichua Indians on the dam gave me a new vision and challenge. They told me I would never visit them in their villages and I knew I had to meet that challenge. The Lord was really drawing my heart toward them. I had become very close to these men. After all, for many months, I was their boss, doctor, pastor, provider and friend. I ate with them, slept with them, cried with them and laughed with them on a daily basis. We lived together eleven months. We even started to think alike. I wanted to see them go on with the Lord and grow in the Lord. I longed to see a strong church in each village.

One Sunday, Monnie and I and all four of our children got into our Land Rover. We went to a small village where we picked up one of the men who had worked with me on the dam project. He told me he could guide us to a village where some of the former workers lived. We were looking for one man in particular. His name was Angel. We traveled many miles over rugged mountain trails and into areas seldom visited by anyone other than Indians. Fortunately, our Land Rover was able to make it up the steep primitive roads and through the deep mud we encountered.

We finally arrived at the small concentration of homes where Angel lived. The Indians were not friendly at first. They had no idea who we were. They are always suspicious of any strangers. We asked an Indian on the trail where Angel lived and he did nothing but point in the direction of Angel's home. The women and children standing in front of their mud huts, just stared blankly at us.

We had driven through Indian villages on weekends before when the whole population of the town was strewn around the streets in complete disarray. Many of the men were passed out from the previous night's drinking. The women, complete with men's-style felt hats and babies slung across their backs, were reeling and they, too, were out of control from the local drink. When the babies cried hard enough to get their attention, they adjusted the sling so the baby lay under their arm far enough to nurse. When the baby was satisfied enough to stop bothering them, they were returned to the woman's back. No one seemed concerned if the baby relieved himself all down his mother's back, or threw up sour milk as babies often do. What a picture! Drunken mothers, reeling along the muddy street, the back of their hand-woven poncho covered in their own child's excrement. This was the life of despair that most of the mountain Indians lived. We were glad to find things a bit better than that in Angel's village when we finally arrived there.

Angel's little hut was set high on the side of the mountain above the trail. Angel came running down the path that led to his home because someone had already told him we were coming to visit him. He was so happy to see us and very surprised that we would ever make the effort to come all that way just to see him! Angel invited us to make the short walk up the mountain path to his home.

Monnie wondered how she would be received by Angel's wife. To Monnie's delight, Angel's wife invited us into their humble little abode. They invited us to sit on a bed in a small room. We were soon surrounded by Angel and their eight children. The single bed and a small table was all that would fit into their single room. Angel's wife ran to their primitive kitchen (a lean-to at the back of the house) and prepared some hard-boiled eggs. She served them from an enameled dish. She also ground some rock salt for us to put on our eggs.

When things settled down, she asked me what I did to cause her husband to change. She was happy because he no longer drank or beat her. He told her that he had accepted Christ as his Savior, but she didn't understand what he meant. So we began explaining what Christ was doing in Angel's life. We assured her that Jesus wanted to save her, also. She was ready, not because of anything we did, but because of Angel's changed life. That afternoon Angel's wife and older children accepted the Lord. The oldest son was the only one in the family who could read, so we gave him a Bible and he promised to read to the rest of the family.

While we talked with Angel and his wife, word was spreading through the area that *Donaldo* (my name in Spanish) was there. Eventually, twenty Indians who accepted the Lord at Loreto Dam gathered and we also fellowshipped with them.

As we left that day, the Christian Indians pleaded with us to come back and help them reach their own people for the Lord. We assured them we would be back. We left with uplifted hearts and with the hope that the Indians would someday have a strong church, starting with these few believers.

However, after holding several meetings in this village, Angel and his family seemed to be the only ones who stood true to the Lord through the persecution their neighbors brought on them. We went back from time to time, always meeting in someone's home, but finally, we decided to show the films on the side of the public school building. That afternoon, we bumped up and down the narrow streets, announcing over a loudspeaker mounted on top of the car that the gospel films would be shown that evening.

By the time it was dark, a good crowd gathered and in the gathering dusk, we could see Indians wending their way down the mountainsides toward the meetingplace. We began the meeting with the first film, then I preached a simple salvation message and (to our amazement) twenty-one Indians accepted the Lord! I knelt and prayed with these new believers. Then we showed another film.

It was a great encouragement to us to see an interest among the mountain Indians that we had not seen before. We began to pray for a real leader among them who could establish a church.

Chapter 7

The Hound of Heaven

Each week, I returned to my duties in the print shop as usual, but that one special little village I had stumbled across while hunting kept coming back to my mind. It was nestled deep in the Andes mountains, but I knew some day I would go back and visit that village even though I had been warned by the Indians that I could be killed if I went back there. Thc Indians told me the name of the village was Oyacachi. They were all frightened of the place because of the rumors they heard about the hostile people who lived there. No one even knew how many people lived in that forbidding valley.

Many of the Ecuadorian Indians are steeped in superstition and fear. Much of what is called worship in these mountains is not true worship because they have never heard the truth about Jesus Christ and what He has done for them.

The story of the Virgin of Quinche is one of the most interesting stories among the mountain people. It was in Oyacachi, the alleged refuge for fugitives, that this virgin appeared and received her fame. Two virgins were supposedly seen by an Indian, playing in a field. Upon seeing them, the Indian invited the virgins into his small hut for a meal. After they ate, the Indians asked them if they would stay in the village forever so the people could worship them. One virgin said she had to leave and immediately disappeared. The other consented to remain. She was transformed into a graven image and became the famous Virgin of Quinche. Her statue was put in a prominent place in the village.

Her fame soon spread to other Indian villages. One day, the Indians of Oyacachi learned of a plot to steal the prized virgin. Being few in number, they felt they could not protect her and quickly made a duplicate, taking the original statue high into the mountains to be hidden. After the imitation was carried away, the Indians brought back the original idol and continued their worship of this virgin. Over the years, it became the custom during certain holidays to carry this famous Virgin of Quinche over the mountains, parading through various neighboring villages. (This custom has not been practiced since the Oyacachi village Indians accepted Jesus Christ as their Savior.)

Two brothers who accepted Christ as their personal Savior while working on the dam project, lived deep in the mountains and knew the actual location of the village. I heard that they knew how to get there. I went to visit them at their mountain home and asked them to guide me to Oyacachi. They said an emphatic, "No." After some time of pleading on my part, they reluctantly agreed to guide me to within three hours' horseback ride of the village. They were adamant about not going any closer. Another Indian who accepted Christ while working on the dam said he would go into the village with me.

We started making plans for the trip. I arranged with our Spanish and Quichua programmers at HCJB to announce several times a day for a full month that a caravan from HCJB would be coming to their village. We even told them what time we would be there. We broadcast this message via radio. The fact that the caravan would actually consist of only two people was never broadcast. Our hope was that these Indians had radios and that they would hear our message and receive us peacefully.

As we approached, I looked at these allegedly dangerous Indians standing in the muddy trail ahead of me. I thought back over all that had transpired over the past two years, bringing me to this point. How the Lord led me to this moment was now very clear in my mind. As a great preacher of the past said, "The hound of heaven" (the Holy Spirit) was searching out these Indians and He had pushed *me* to go and find them. It was *imperative* that I go and share the gospel message with them.

Don and Companion on Their Way to Oyacachi

With a prayer under our breath, we approached the Indians standing in the trail. To our delight, they were smiling and seemed happy to see us. They had heard the broadcast and were eagerly awaiting our arrival. They were amazed that anyone would actually come all that long way to visit them. We were overjoyed to be received so enthusiastically—it was a great relief. We were invited into the first little hut on the trail and served hard-boiled eggs. Hard-boiled eggs are about the best food the Indians can offer anyone. There is really no way to alter the taste of a hard-boiled egg and, because it is still in the shell, you can be rather confident that it is clean.

Let me tell you what I mean: Some months later, I was invited to a weekend Bible conference in the mountains. After traveling for several hours, I finally arrived at the village. It was about four o'clock in the afternoon. The Indian women were preparing soup for the meal we were to have that night after the evening service. The men had just killed a goat and it was hanging by its hind feet between two poles. They removed the innards of the goat and cut them into little pieces, throwing them into the large pot where the soup was cooking. That pot held about fifty gallons of soup. The pot was placed over a raging fire in the open air near the Indian hut. The women added rice, noodles, potatoes and "other things" to the goat meat. We were expecting about 300 Indians for the conference so they had to prepare lots of soup. Everyone was invited to eat after the service.

Preparing Goat Soup

Our typical Indian service lasted until about 10:30 at night. The soup had been cooking since four o'clock in the afternoon. After the service we all made our way to the small hut where the food was being served. They gave me a large bowl of this goat soup. I always tried to eat at least *some* of the food the Indians gave me so I wouldn't offend them. However, this soup was something else. I lifted a spoonful of soup toward my mouth but the smell was so bad that my stomach said, "Don't do it!" I tried again, but I began to gag.

I thought maybe if I ate some bread or boiled potatoes to get a different taste in my mouth, then I could eat the soup. So, I prayed, "God, please help me eat this soup." Slowly, I raised the spoonful of soup toward my mouth and *even God* would not help me !

I made my way out of the hut, out under the stars and away from where most of the Indians were eating. When I thought I was alone and that no one was watching, I threw the soup into a corn-field. Just as I turned around, a smiling Indian standing right in front of me, watching, asked, "Would you like some more?" I politely said, "No, I've had plenty!" That is why I say a hard-boiled egg is the best food an Indian can give you.

There in Oyacachi, we thoroughly enjoyed the hard-boiled eggs and after telling the Indian family goodbye, we mounted our horses and continued down the trail toward the village. We hadn't gone very far before we saw another hut and some Indians standing in front of it. They were just as friendly as the first family and invited us into their hut. The father had just shot a deer and it was hanging by the open fire. He cut off two large pieces of deer meat and quickly prepared some deer steaks for us. The steaks were cooked over the open fire and were delicious.

The husband prepared the steaks because his wife was very sick. She had been running a high fever for over a week. She was lying on a mat on the dirt floor, covered with a badly-soiled blanket. They had her near the open cooking fire. I had taken some aspirin along for myself, so I gave her two aspirin with water. I then gave her husband four more pills and told him to give her two more when the sun went down, and the last two when the sun came up. They had no electricity, and no clocks so I couldn't tell them what time to take the medicine.

Again, we mounted our horses and headed down the trail toward the village. Our attention was drawn to two men who were busy threshing oats by hand—the same way it was done in Bible days at the threshing floor. In a hut, a group of women and children were sitting on the dirt-packed floor, shelling *habas* (lima beans). They just stared at us as we passed by.

We finally saw the village and lots of Indians—men, women and children, waiting for us. After dismounting and greeting all the people gathered there to welcome us, we met the leader of the village. He said, "There is one man you must meet." He quickly sent a young man running off to bring this special man back.

While we were waiting for the men to return, we observed that the Indians lived in little huts with low walls and high thatched roofs. The huts were scattered across the village site. They were not in any particular order. The Indians almost immediately started bringing us gifts. The men brought us hand-carved wooden bowls and large hand-carved wooden spoons. The older women brought us fresh eggs. I never could figure out what they thought we would do with all these fresh eggs since we were on horseback. Later, we did learn how to transport them—we asked someone to boil them for us and they travelled very nicely and made a nice lunch for us while we were on the trail.

The Indians were very shy and gave us the gifts only if they thought no one was watching. Taking the gifts from beneath their ponchos, they slipped them to us without saying a word. Then, they just stepped back and smiled. We *never* expected this kind of a reception.

Soon the messenger came running back with another young man close behind. The second young man was very excited to see us. He informed us that he was a believer. He accepted the Lord in that remote village while listening to HCJB radio. He eagerly asked us if we could have a church service. Since he was the only believer in the entire village, he wanted all his people to hear about the Lord.

That afternoon all the Indians were invited to the first church service ever to be held in this remote village. The Indian believer who accompanied me to the village gave his testimony after which I preached. After the message, I gave an invitation to anyone who wanted to be saved and sixteen Indians, both men and women, accepted Christ.

First Church Service Ever in the Village of Oyacachi

The leader of the village invited us to eat and sleep in his little hut that night. He had no beds, so I rolled my sleeping bag out on the floor. My Indian companion slept on the dirt floor with his poncho thrown over him. At least we had a roof over our heads.

We slowly realized that the way had been prepared for us because the highland Indians listened to the radio. They listened to HCJB because it was the only station they could get so high up in the mountains. HCJB broadcasts by shortwave radio and covers every inch of the mountains. Owning a radio was a status symbol among the Indians. Anyone who didn't have a radio was considered to be a "nobody".

The Japanese did us all a great favor when they began making cheap shortwave radios. They made a three- and a five-band radio, but the Indians wanted the best, so they purchased the five-band radio even though all they could get on any band was HCJB. I jokingly said to them, "Well, at least you have a choice of which band you want to hear us on!" As they walked the mountain trails, they carried their radios close to their ears. Many times, they were turned off or else they had the volume all the way up. You could hear them coming down the trail from far away.

One Indian who was hostile to the gospel was asked by a Gospel Missionary Union missionary why he was listening to HCJB. He said, "They are the only ones that speak my language." He referred to the fact that only HCJB offered programs in the Quichua language—the other stations only offered Spanish programs.

As these isolated Indians were enlightened by listening to the radio, they began to seek more education—and they were more open to the gospel. The more the gospel penetrated these mountains, however, the more the opposition grew. The State church began to see their power over these Indians slipping away. The opposition came in the form of threats, stonings, beatings with clubs, homes were burned, crops were destroyed, and believers were killed as were their animals. Some families even disowned their family members who became Christians.

The first believers had to be strong to continue in the faith under these conditions. We knew that only God could keep them steadfast. One Indian told me with tears running down his cheeks, "They have killed my animals, destroyed my crops and they tried to burn my home." Then, a smile crept across his face and he said, "But they can't take away my God, can they?" I wondered if I could be so strong under the same circumstances.

I believed from early on that the best way to gather a crowd was to use gospel films. A dear friend, Bill Mitchell, and his wife, Joyce, purchased a movie projector, a small power plant and some gospel films for us to use in the villages. We started with the life of Christ and always showed the first and the last of the twelve-film series. Those showed the birth of Christ and His resurrection.

When the Indians heard about Mary, you could hear them murmuring, "Maria! Maria!" That made them more willing to hear our message. After this first film, I usually preached to them and then showed the second film. To close, I gave another short message and the invitation. The results were unbelievable.

At first, so many Indians responded that I made them go back and sit down (on the floor or on the ground in an open field sometimes). Then I explained again about the gospel and told them that they were in for persecution if they accepted Christ —they might be stoned, beaten, or even killed. I almost tried to talk them out of becoming Christians. I only wanted the ones who were serious about this decision to come forward, but when I asked, "Now, how many want to come forward to accept Christ?" even more came than before.

I asked some of them why they were so ready to respond to the gospel the first time they heard it, and they told me it was not the first time they had heard the gospel. They had heard the gospel for years over HCJB. This was just the first time anyone had given them a chance to respond!

The mountain Indians were ready to accept Christ. All I did was reap the harvest. Many missionaries had sown the seed—that had been very hard. Others had watered the seed and that too, was difficult, but I had great joy in reaping the harvest that God so graciously allowed me to see.

There in Oyacachi the next morning, we drank coffee and ate homemade bread. We prepared for the trip home. The Indians told us there was a shorter way to the village from the other direction ... it was only an eight-hour horseback ride. They had pastured our horses. They brought them back early in the morning and saddled them for us. Almost all the Indians who lived in the village came to see us off. They brought us more gifts and we prayed with the Indians before leaving. Our prayer was simple—we prayed that *all* of the nearly 200 Indians living in this remote village and in the area would come to know Christ as their Savior.

I thought as I left, "What if I had not obeyed the voice of God? What if I had not come to this village? What if I had said, 'It is too dangerous'?" What a blessing I would have missed. God wanted to *bless me* with this opportunity to minister in Jesus' name.

As we rode back, we came to the home of the sick woman. To our surprise, she was out in the field hoeing her corn. The aspirin was like a wonder drug. The Indians never had any medicine before. The family kept thanking us for making their mother well. They called me "doctor". I joked, "I'm not even a nurse."

We made it back to the Indians who were waiting on the trail in the mountains before the ten o'clock deadline. We were thrilled with what the Lord had done in the village of Oyacachi. However, we did not look forward to the two long, hard days of riding across the mountains on horseback over the miserable trail. We knew the rugged terrain that lay before us—to say nothing of the wind, cold, sleet and rain we would encounter.

After a total of five days on the trail (which included more than 32 hours on horseback), I arrived home safe and sound, rejoicing in the Lord and sharing my experiences with my family.

Chapter 8

God Gave the Increase

Some of the men from Oyacachi visited an evangelical church in the city of Cayambe. The pastor was excited to hear that they were new believers from that distant village of Oyacachi. They offered to provide horses for him to visit the village, and he took them up on their offer and visited their village. After his visit into the village, he sent greetings via HCJB radio to the believers in the village. He thanked them for the trip and for their hospitality. When I heard him send greetings to the believers at Oyacachi over the radio, I decided I should meet this pastor.

One Sunday morning Monnie, the children and I traveled three hours to the city of Cayambe, north of Quito. We located the church and met Jaime Lomas, the pastor. He asked me to preach that Sunday morning, and I did. After the church service, we went to his house for lunch where we enjoyed a wonderful lunch prepared by Jaime's wife who is a wonderful cook. We compared notes on Oyacachi and decided we should visit the village together. He invited the Oyacachi believers to sleep in the church whenever they came to market. Because of this, he was able to arrange for horses to take us into the village. We set a date for this visit to the village and we started making plans for the trip.

I drove to Cayambe on a Friday night and stayed all night with Jaime. Some of the men from Oyacachi had come out with the horses to guide us to the village. They were also sleeping at the church. The next morning after breakfast, at six o'clock, we all loaded into the Land Rover, along with our baggage, to make the two-hour trip to the end of the road. Other Indians who stayed with the horses, were waiting for us.

After eight long, hard hours on the treacherous trail, we arrived in Oyacachi. We were soaked to the skin from the rain and (to say the least), we were cold and tired from the trip. The Indians were very understanding and took us to a hut where they prepared some hot coffee. We changed into dry clothes and sat around the open fire and talked. The women prepared something for us to eat. They mixed up some bread dough and rolled it into what looked like tubes. Then they pinched off a piece and formed it into a donut. They cooked it in hot grease over an open fire. When it was golden brown they took it out of the grease and served it to us. It was the best Indian food I have ever eaten. We were given a corner of the hut to spread out our sleeping bags and we went to bed.

Even though there was a concentration of huts that made up the village, every family had a portion of land. Some ran cattle on their land while others were farmers. They were very private people who were self-sufficient for the most part. They purchased only rice, rock salt, coffee, candles and oil for their little lamps at the market. Some of the men carved crude wooden bowls of all sizes from logs they brought up from the jungle. A trip to the jungle took two days each way on horseback. They sold the wooden bowls at the market in Cayambe which was at least a ten-hour walk from their home.

Each family had their own hut and they lived a very primitive lifestyle. They had no beds, tables, chairs, stoves and no electricity—all things we consider to be basic necessities. They might have one change of clothes each. There was no source of entertainment. The man of the house probably had a horse. The women were expected to work all day in the field as well as to do the cooking, washing clothes in a nearby stream and caring for the children. There were many children even though the infant mortality rate was 97 per cent. If a child could make it past one or two years old, they had a good chance of living. It truly was "survival of the fittest".

The little huts always consisted of only one room. Some were a little larger than others, but inside they were all the same. In one corner there was a straw mat on the dirt floor for sleeping and in another corner they stored their supplies such as rice, salt, corn. The women cooked over an open fire in the middle of the little hut. The pots and pans, black from the smoke, were hung from the ceiling. Every home had guinea pigs running around—sometimes dozens of them. The dirt floor was swept with a branch of a tree or bush. The sides of the hut were made of hand-cut boards that stood side by side and were fastened to the thatched roof. The thatched roof always had a small hole right at the peak to allow the smoke to escape. The inside of the hut is always black from the smoke. Water had to be brought from a nearby stream. Of course, there were no bathroom facilities. One night when it was raining hard and we were getting ready for bed, Jaime said to me, "Just going to the restroom here is really a major problem!"

The next morning, Jaime and I started going from hut to hut to visit the Indians. They all wanted to feed us something. One young couple wanted us to dedicate their one-day-old baby girl to the Lord, so Jaime and I prayed with them in a small dedication service. It was great to see the growth of these believers in just a few months. They had named the first believer in the village as pastor. He told us there were 30 who wanted to be baptized on Sunday. These Indians had been busy leading their friends and family to the Lord.

Since they had no church building, we held our Sunday church service in the open air. Fortunately it wasn't raining. After the service, the congregation (which consisted of nearly the whole village) made their way up the trail to some hot springs. There was a large pool of hot water. What a blessing! I was afraid I would have to go into the ice-cold river water! We all gathered on the banks of the pool and sang hymns. The ones to be baptized gave their testimonies and Jaime and I both entered the water and took turns baptizing the believers.

During our stay in the village, 20 more Indians accepted Christ. We were seeing a strong church being built before our very eyes! We stayed two days this time and before we left, the believers showed us where they were going to build their new church. They already had permission from the village leaders to build on that spot—it was right in the middle of the village. They were going to build the church out of rock that was nearby.

After a word of prayer and a few words of encouragement, we mounted our horses for the eight-hour horseback ride back to the Land Rover. I then took Jaime home (which took two hours) and then it was three hours back to Quito and my family.

I always arrived home dirty and tired. Monnie was always waiting for me with a freshly baked pie and while I soaked in the bath tub, she brought me hot coffee and pie. We talked about my trip and the meetings.

Jaime and I made several more trips into Oyacachi and each time, more Indians accepted the Lord and were baptized. On one of these trips, I took my oldest daughter, Shari, who was seventeen years old. We reached the end of the road and when the Indians saw her, they were not too sure she could make it. I told them it was okay and that she would make it. This particular trip was really hard since it rained all the way and when we reached the pass at about 15,000 feet high, the sleet was blowing so hard the horses didn't want to go on. We kept prodding them on and once we were over the pass it was a little better, but the cold and wet were relentless. The driving rain made the trail almost impassable. It was quite a trip for Shari. Her first trip into the village was really something to remember and even now (25 years later), she remembers it as a highlight of her growing up.

Even with two years' experience visiting remote villages, when we arrived at Oyacachi that day, the Indians could not believe that a little "gringa" (white girl) could make that trip in that kind of weather. Shari made friends with many of the young girls in the village. The next day, an Indian lady came to the village and she wanted to see Shari. She said, "When I got to the pass yesterday, the wind and sleet were so bad that I turned back. How did you make it?" Because of this, Shari was looked upon like some super lady. Of course, I always knew she was!

By this time, however, the church was finished and we were planning a full week of celebration. The Indians built the church without any outside help. We never gave them money or supplies for the church. That made it *theirs* and they were proud of the fact that they had not required help ... so were we.

I told them I wanted to furnish part of the food for the dedication of the church. I purchased 400 pounds of food to be sent into the village a few weeks before the dedication.

The Indians were making all the preparations for the dedication. The believers there planned the entire week even though Jaime and I would be there to preach and teach. I also arranged for Dr. Douce, a missionary doctor, to hold a clinic all week for the Indians. My daughter, Shari, really wanted to go back for the dedication service and all the Indians wanted her to come, also. I knew there would be games, so prizes would be needed. I purchased several Bibles, pencils, ballpoint pens, notebooks and 20 pounds of various kinds of candy for prizes.

The Indians were busy working on the trail, so the caravan would have an easier trip to the village. Others were preparing housing for all of us. Some were planning the menu for the week. Still others were planning the games. We needed a lot of horses to get us all to the village.

When we arrived at the end of the road, we found 25 Indians and 15 pack horses ready to escort Jaime, Shari, Dr. Douce, myself and others into this isolated mountain village. The Indians were busy packing the horses with a portable power plant, gas for the plant, 13 gospel films, Bibles, New Testaments, songbooks, medical supplies and the prizes for the games. Besides all that, each of us had our personal gear such as sleeping bags, dry clothes and anything else we felt we needed to make the week a success. The 16mm movie projector was carried in by an eighty-year-old man. He was very careful so that it wouldn't be damaged in any way. With such a large caravan, it took longer than usual to reach the village. The trail was muddy. Some of the pack horses sank in up to their bellies and had to be unloaded and pulled out of the mud, which reminded me of the Loreto Dam project!

Pack Horses on Their Way to Oyacachi

All in all, it was a good trip even though the ones making the trip for the first time couldn't believe the trail. On our arrival, we greeted the believers in the village, had supper, and then bedded down for the night.

The next morning the pastor showed us the schedule. We were to have a Bible study every morning and afternoon. Every evening, we were to have gospel films, followed by a worship service. One day was set aside for games and a special meal for the whole village and anyone else who chose to come to the Christian "fiesta". These Indians were all saved out of the State church where they were used to a week-long fiesta to celebrate their saints' day. It was always a week of drinking and dancing. Everyone got drunk and there was a lot of immorality. Now that these Indians were Christians, they wanted to show everyone that they could have *a great time* without the liquor and sin. They wanted it to be a testimony to the entire area. The Holy Spirit was truly working in their hearts.

The little church building was rather crude. It was built from rocks stacked one on top of the other. On one side, they had an opening for a door, but there was no actual door, and there were two holes which served as windows. There was no glass in the windows. There were no benches in the church, but they had covered the dirt floor with parramo grass. They had hand carried in tin for the roof. It served very well for a meeting place. And most important, they had built it themselves!

We ran an extension cord for electric lights. Many of these Indians had never seen an electric light. Most of the rest had only rarely seen electric lights. They were all very interested and excited to see what would happen that night. We took a white bed sheet and fastened it to the wall at one end of the church. This would serve as a screen for the films. We ran a long extension cord to the small power plant. The plant had to be some distance from the church so the noise from the plant didn't drown out what was being said in church.

I will never forget the first night. When we started the plant and the lights went on, all the Indians laughed nervously. The church was wall-to-wall Indians, all sitting on the floor. The entire area has about 200 Indians living in and around the village. The church was so full that no one could move. Shari and I were on the outside, looking in through one of the windows. When the first film was shown, we could see the reaction of the Indians. Since none of them had never seen a film before, they were very embarrassed and hid their faces in their hands. They thought the people on the screen were looking at them and they felt conspicuous. They opened their hands in front of their eyes, just a little, to peek to see if the people on the screen were still watching them and then they quickly closed their hands again. Shari and I stood outside laughing between ourselves. I told Shari, "We will have to show this film over because no one is watching it." It wasn't long, however, until they were all watching and enjoying the films we brought for them to see.

The Indians provided Dr. Douce with a little hut to set up his clinic. He asked Shari if she would like to help by acting as his nurse. She was more than happy to help. At the end of the first day, they had only one patient. Dr. Douce told me he had never been in a village with so few patients. Usually he had more patients than he could handle. With tongue in cheek, I told him that in this village the people are either very healthy or they were dead. There was no in between! However, as the Indians lost their fear of a doctor, they began going to him with minor problems.

Friday was set aside for the games and the big fiesta. That morning, we all gathered in a clearing beside the church. A very long pole was lying on the ground. The Indians fastened many prizes on one end of the pole. The prizes consisted of a Bible, notebooks, ballpoint pens, a large bag of candy, fruits and some money among other things. After making sure the prizes were all secure, they took pig lard and greased the pole from top to bottom. The pole was then set in a deep hole and made secure. Anyone who could climb the pole and reach the prizes could have everything they could get off the top before they lost their hold and slid back down the pole. The women and girls never tried because they all wear skirts and are very modest. All the Indians laughed when someone got part way up the pole and, in spite of all their effort, slid back down the pole.

Climbing the Greased Pole

The first few never had a chance because of all the grease on the pole. Each person could go a little higher as the grease was wiped off on their pant legs as they climbed up the pole. Finally a young man made it to the top. He was smart, and rather than grabbing one thing, he got hold of the tip top of the pole and held himself in place with one hand as he removed each prize with the other hand and threw it to the ground.

They also had games for the children. They had foot races, sack races and many other games. Each child got a prize for winning. Some never won but Shari and I felt sorry for them and we got several bags of candy and gathered all the children around and started throwing the candy high into the air, one handful at a time. The children were running everywhere to get the candy. All the adults just stood and laughed because the children were having such a good time. We made sure all the children, even the very small ones, got some candy. The mothers were especially happy when the little ones got a prize.

Scampering for Candy

The men prepared a game to be played on horseback. They stretched a rope between two poles, five to six feet off the ground and tied ten wooden rings on the rope. Each ring was hanging by a string about twelve inches long. The men mounted their horses and with a pencil in one hand, they rode on a dead run trying to get their pencil through a ring. If they succeeded, the ring came off on their pencil with a long ribbon streaming from the ring. I have no idea where the ribbon came from. I just know that it happened. It was fun to see these riders make their attempts, and everyone cheer when someone got a ring. The most amusing part was when a well-known Indian came on a donkey that wouldn't run and he still missed! The Indians thought that was very funny.

The next game was open to both men, women and children. They covered a young pig with lard and turned him loose. The person who could catch him and bring him to the judge got a prize. It was funny to see someone coming with the pig ... only to have him slip out of their arms and run away. It was good to see them having fun, laughing and having a great time. That is exactly what they wanted to show everyone. They wanted the others in the village and surrounding area to know that you don't need liquor to have a good time.

After the games we all went to eat. The women had prepared a variety of food and lots of it. The Indians always have soup first. Then they had a large bowl of rice, topped with pieces of meat. After that, they served such things as boiled potatoes, bread, and fresh corn on the cob among other things.

A Feast Was Enjoyed By All

Since we were special guests, they gave us a big bowl of rice topped with a guinea pig. It still had its head and feet. This is considered a delicacy and given only to special people. At that point, I wished I weren't so special! Times like these were when I considered a dog to be man's best friend. They are always around and usually you can slip a guinea pig to them, or at least part of it. The guinea pig meat is not too bad, but it is quite tough and it's hard to eat with those big brown eyes looking back at you. It kind of gets to you. The Indians suck the brain and eyeballs out of the head and find them quite delicious.

The evening service was attended by almost everyone in the village. Some of the Indians really hated the Christians, but they liked the films, so they came to the services. Later, many of them accepted the Lord.

Baptismal Service in the Hot Springs Pool

On Saturday, we had a baptismal service at the hot springs. After singing and testimonies, Jaime and I baptized 25 Indians. It was such a joy to see these big, strong Indians with weather-beaten faces, cry as they gave testimony of how the Lord had saved them and the joy they now had. Their living **conditions did not change**, they didn't build a better home or acquire more land, but **they were content** to have the joy of the Lord and nothing else.

We all went back to the church to attend the first Christian wedding ever to take place in Oyacachi. The bride was dressed in a white dress and the groom was dressed in nice, clean pants and shirt. I had the privilege of performing the wedding ceremony. The service didn't last long. By law, they must have their papers in order. When the paperwork is finished, they are legally married. This couple wanted to get married as Christians in the church for a testimony to everyone and to ask God's blessing on the home they were about to establish. After the wedding, we were all invited to their home for a wedding feast.

Parade of Believers Through the Village

These Indians had been saved out of a church that paraded their saints through the village and so they wanted to parade their new-found faith through the village as they had done in years past with their saints. So they planned a parade to the new church.

The pastor led the parade with a large open Bible. Behind him came two men carrying communion cups on a tray. They were followed by two young girls carrying the Ecuadorian and the Christian flags. Then came Jaime and myself. Shari and Dr. Douce followed us. Then came the elders two by two, the deacons two by two and all the other believers in the village followed them, two abreast. We all had Bibles held high above our heads so the unsaved could see them. Each pair was about twenty feet apart. It made quite a sight as we paraded around the village. The parade ended at the church building and we all entered for the morning service and the dedication service.

Dedication of the New Church

Before the message, I had the privilege of dedicating 12 babies to the Lord. In reality, the couples were dedicating *themselves* to the Lord, promising to bring up the child in a Christian home, and to pray for their early salvation.

After the preaching service we all gathered outside, formed a circle and a dedication service was held. Several of the Christian Indians spoke and gave their testimonies. I closed with prayer, asking God to bless this little church and everyone who worshipped here. We all went back into the church and joined in partaking of the Lord's supper.

Overflowing Church Service

The week was a great time of Bible studies and fellowship. God gave us 20 more decisions for the Lord during the week. Now we were ready to leave the village again. We knew the trip out would be almost as hard as the trip in, but we were leaving with joyful hearts.

Jaime, the pastor from Cayambe, continued to visit the village of Oyacachi from time to time. I was glad he could do that because it allowed me time to go to other places. However, every year, on the anniversary of the church, we both went back to the village for special services. Each anniversary trip lasted six days and always included Bible studies, preaching, Gospel films, baptisms, baby dedications, weddings and more Indians accepted the Lord.

On one trip to Oyacachi, I was interrupted twice during the baptismal service by Indians who wanted to accept Christ. They didn't even want to wait until we finished the service. On another occasion, a father came forward with his son while I was preaching, and asked if his son could accept the Lord at that very moment. God was truly working among these Indians. One morning, we were having a baby dedication service and the pastor asked the mother the name of her baby and to my surprise she replied, "His name is *Santo Donaldo*," translated Saint Donald. I was honored that the family thought enough of me to name their son after me.

Another time, after I had given a message on the Lord's supper, the Holy Spirit spoke to many Christians. For almost three hours, we witnessed stout, rugged Indians confessing their failures to the Lord and to one another with tears running down their ruddy, wind-chapped cheeks. Men and women were crying and hugging each other. After that, we served the Lord's supper.

In the first five years of the existence of this church, the believers started five other churches in the mountains and jungles of Ecuador. By this time, most of the inhabitants in and around Oyacachi had made a decision to follow Christ.

Eight years after the first church was built, the village of Oyacachi had to be relocated because of mudslides. One night, after lots of rain, half the mountain slid to within a few yards of the village. The mudslide was so large it dammed up the river, forming a lake. The Indians were fearful that the other half of the mountain would slide down and wipe out their village. So they decided to move the entire village up the valley about an hour's horseback ride. Each family dismantled their little hut, carried it to the new location and put it back together again. Since the church was made of stones, it could not be moved. A new and larger church was built at the new location. This church was built of wood.

As the gospel began to spread across the mountains, so did the opposition to the gospel. Unsaved Indians were encouraged to attack the believers in hopes of stopping the spread of the gospel. We were warned by the Christians that some of the unsaved Indians were going to attack us and stop us from going back to Oyacachi. Since we always left our Land Rover at the end of the road with no protection, we were fearful it would be destroyed by these hostile Indians. So we rented a truck to take us and all our equipment to the end of the road. We hoped they would not recognize us in a different vehicle. The mud was so deep the truck could not make it to the end of the road and the horses had to be brought down to the truck and loaded for the trip. Using the truck for the trip worked because we faced no opposition. It was nice to see the new church building and to fellowship with the Indians again. Fourteen Indians accepted the Lord during that stay.

Our daughter Shari and her husband, Paul Salzman, were accepted as missionaries with HCJB World Radio and they came to Ecuador with their two children, Peggy and Scott. When the Indians at Oyacachi heard that Shari was back in Ecuador, they wanted to see her. Monnie agreed to keep Peggy and Scott and we made plans to go back to Oyacachi. The trip to the village was still as hard as ever and Paul had never been on horseback before or over any mountain trails before. His horse slipped and fell on his foot, making the rest of the trip difficult for him.

The Indians were thrilled to see Shari again and to meet Paul. Several of the young girls Shari knew were also married and it made for a great reunion for them. Even though they had a great time and a wonderful opportunity for sharing, Shari and Paul were glad to get back to their children ... and I think grandma was happy to turn the grandchildren over to their parents.

In 1983, the mission asked my wife and me to return to the States to do representation work across the entire nation. After three years of representation, we returned to Ecuador to spend a few months of re-orientation at the station in Quito.

Shortly after our arrival back in Ecuador, the pastor of the church in Oyacachi heard we were back. He immediately invited me to the dedication of the new church building. He told me that 98 percent of all the people in and around Oyacachi were now Christians. He said I had to come to the dedication because I was the first missionary to ever visit the village nearly 14 years earlier. He wanted me to see how God had blessed through the years.

The believers made great plans for the dedication of the new building. They asked the wife of the president of Ecuador to come. She was a fine Christian lady and she accepted the invitation to attend the dedication service. She was to be flown to the village by helicopter for only a couple of hours in order to be the honored guest during the service. Because she was coming, many government officials also agreed to attend. Of course, with the president's wife and all the government officials coming, the news media also wanted to be there. They sent out news reporters and a TV camera crew. Many Christian leaders and workers from around Ecuador also planned to attend.

It was a foggy, cold, damp day and the wind was blowing a gale, as we prepared to leave from the top of the mountain for the seven-hour trip into the village. The Indians came to meet us with 40 horses to take us and our equipment over the winding, treacherous trail to the small Indian village.

About halfway to the village, we heard over the radio that the president of Ecuador had been abducted by some military generals. The news reporters became very excited and immediately wanted to return to Quito, but the Indians wouldn't lead them back for fear they would miss the dedication of the church.

As we descended the mountain and as the village came into view, I could see the large, new church with its bright red roof towering over the small mud huts. A beautiful stained-glass window formed a cross on the front of the building. The sight was truly a testimony to all who entered the village.

The building was made of cement blocks and had a cement floor overlaid with ceramic tile. The framework was made of steel beams. Every window was of stained glass. All this had to be carried in over the rugged trail over which we had just come. The Indians, themselves, made the hand-carved beautiful wooden pulpit. I was amazed to see the church furnished with brand new wooden pews, enough to seat around 400 people. Pews are something you seldom find in an Indian church.

Because the president of Ecuador had been abducted, his wife was unable to attend the service. (A week or so later he was released, unharmed.) I was privileged to cut the ribbon, opening the new church. The Indians seemed to be thrilled to see me again and during the dedication service, they presented me with a beautiful hand-carved wooden plate to commemorate the occasion.

As I ministered in preaching and teaching, my heart was warmed as I saw the fruit that God had given over the years. It was truly gratifying that the church was going on and growing. This church in the truest sense is an indigenous church. The pastor was the first believer and the Christians built their own building. They asked for no outside help at all. God has blessed them and they have given themselves and their money to the work of the Lord. I was humbled and grateful to the Lord to have been used to witness and preach the gospel to them.

Chapter 9

Danger, Deprivation and ... More Danger

Most of the time Monnie, for several reasons, did not go on preaching trips that necessitated staying overnight. The Indian culture was so completely different and living conditions were really primitive. Sleeping arrangements were bad. Everyone—women, men and children—slept in the same room, usually packed in so close that there was not even room for everyone to lie down. Some of the Indians slept sitting up against the walls of the mud huts.

There were no sanitary facilities. The woods or jungle surrounding the area was the only way to find any privacy at all and even then, there were always Indians watching everything we did and every move we made. The Indian women and men had no problem with bodily functions. They relieved themselves wherever they happened to be when the time came, out in the open if necessary, totally without social embarrassment or any thought of sanitary consideration.

On one occasion, Monnie and all four of our children accompanied me to a jungle meeting. We drove twelve hours over a bumpy, dirt road to a small church deep in the Ecuadorian jungle. The pastor's house was situated on stilts in the middle of a clearing which was about 30 yards square. The jungle was like a wall on all four sides. Monnie developed amoebic dysentery and sought privacy in the jungle for sanitation reasons. The dysentery got so bad, we had to return to Quito. I told the pastor I would return in a few weeks for the meetings.

When I arrived the second time at the pastor's home, he invited me in and decided that he would catch a chicken and have his wife cook it for the evening meal. The chicken ran like crazy and the Indians there were all laughing and chasing it about the clearing, trying to catch it. The pastor's dog got excited about the whole thing and he started chasing after the chicken, too. About then, the chicken darted into the jungle with the dog right behind it. The chicken immediately came running back out of the jungle, but the dog did not appear! One of the men ran over to the edge of the jungle, peered in, turned around and said to the pastor, "Your dog is dead!"

"No, he isn't," replied the pastor, shaking his head and laughing.

The man said again, "Yes, he's dead all right."

And the dog was dead! A poisonous snake lay right inside the jungle wall where the chicken went in. The snake must have been coiled to strike the chicken when he came running past, missed the chicken and got the dog instead. It killed the dog, just that quickly! And then I realized in horror that was the exact spot where Monnie entered the jungle just a few short weeks before! We thanked the Lord for His protection during those days.

We did make many one-day trips with the whole family. Monnie and I felt our children were just as much missionaries as we were, and we wanted them to enter into the work of the Lord and experience firsthand the excitement of what God was doing among the Indians. God was calling out *"a people for His name"*, and we didn't want to miss it.

* *

We knew that God was with us at the village of Cachi Alto. We arrived at the village early, at approximately four o'clock, in the afternoon. On the road into the village, I picked up some believers going to the meeting where we would speak that evening. As we made our way up the mountain, we stopped to talk to an Italian man who lived among the Indians. He was trying to form communes in that area. He appeared very friendly and told me there were a lot of people waiting for us at the end of the road in the plaza. What he didn't tell me was that he had arranged for fourteen communities to get together to attack us—that's who was waiting for us.

Since we were early getting to the village, there were *only* two to three hundred Indians waiting for us—we found out later that over five hundred Indians showed up for the attack. These hostile Indians were waiting all right, but not for the meeting! They were armed with freshly cut clubs, machetes, shotguns, shovels, picks, hoes and rocks. These drunken Indians blocked the road and forced our car to a halt. When I saw all that, I knew we were in trouble and I told them, "We came in *peace* and we will leave in *peace*." We hoped it wouldn't be in *pieces*! The believers tried to reason with the mob while I turned the car around.

One of the hostile Indians fired a shotgun into the air which made the crowd very nervous. They began pushing and hitting the believers. I told my friends to slowly get back into the car. I had a feeling that the minute I began to roll, they would pounce on the car. The hubbub continued to increase. I thought all the believers were in the car, so I put the car in low gear, popped the clutch and gave it the gas. As we sped away, the unsaved Indians started beating on the car and throwing rocks at the car, just as I had suspected.

We hadn't gone very far when I was told that four of the believers didn't make it into the car. It was too late to stop. I could see the Indians chasing the car. We had to make a big switchback on the mountain road and some of the hostile Indians were trying to get to the other side of the canyon to stop us as we passed by. We were able to outrun them. Other Indians, making their way up the mountain, tried to hit the car with whatever they had in their hands.

When we began to think that we were fairly safe, we met two Indians coming up the road. One had a large club in his hand and the other looked as though he had a rock in his hand. I thought if I could get close enough to the one with the rock, he couldn't throw it very hard. So, I swerved the car toward him and he came running toward the car. Just as we approached him, I realized he had a **revolver** in his hand, and it was pointed right at my head! As we passed him, his hand hit the rear view mirror, deflecting the gun, and causing the bullet to make a deep indention in the car door right by my side. This had to be God's hand of protection!

Knowing that it was impossible to return and rescue the other four believers without help, we made our way to the nearest village and asked the police to help us. They told us they had only three policemen and they felt it would be wise for us to go to a larger town for help. There, after some delay, seventeen soldiers were dispatched to help us rescue the four Christian Indians. The soldiers with their automatic rifles and ammunition, were loaded into three vehicles. Their orders were to not fire unless fired upon, in which case they were to use live ammunition. Just two years before, the soldiers killed twelve Indians in an uprising and I knew they would not hesitate to do the same thing now.

The road was dark and dusty as we made our way up the mountain to the small Indian village. After we made inquiries, we were told there were three Indians dying beside an Indian hut about a mile off the road. Eight of the armed soldiers and I arrived at the Indian hut to find three badly-beaten Indians sitting on the outside, leaning against a mud wall. They did, indeed, look as if they were dying. Their heads had been split open. One Indian had been shot in the hand by a shotgun. As gently as we could, we carried the three injured Christians to the road and got them into the cars. We rushed them to the nearest hospital nearly two hours away. They groaned all the way from the pain they were suffering from their injuries. They had multiple fractures and broken bones and it was evident that they had been unmercifully beaten.

The fourth Indian was more fortunate. He had been clubbed in the head and had a big cut across his nose. His body was covered with welts which he had received when he was beaten with a rawhide whip, but he escaped while they were beating the other three Indians. The following day, the hostile and savage Indians were still drinking their homemade liquor and celebrating their so-called "victory". They were making plans to burn down the homes of the Christian Indians who lived in the area. The Italian told me, face to face, that the one they really wanted to hurt was me, but they failed as God was watching over me and He had other plans.

Since the Christians could identify their attackers and they knew the identity of the man who shot at me, we took them to court. We won the case and several of the hostile Indians went to jail. The Italian went free even though he had planned the entire attack according to some of the unbelieving Indians who took part in the attack.

The devil *"is a roaring lion, walking about, seeking whom he may devour"*, but it is also true that God is faithful and He works in strange ways. The man who shot at me accepted Christ in prison and hundreds of the other Indians who were in on the attack accepted the Lord within the following year. Now there are two thriving churches in that very area. We never heard what happened to the Italian as he disappeared. The church always grows under persecution because the unsaved see the power of God in the believers and they want that power for themselves.

* * * * * * * * * * * * * * * * * * * *

I was busy packing the car for my trip to a remote mountain village. I needed a checklist to make sure I didn't forget anything. The small power plant, the projector, a long extension cord, the white bed sheet to serve as a movie screen, Bibles to be sold (cheaply, but results are better if they buy rather than get them free), tracts, my sleeping bag and dry clothes were just some of the necessary items. One time, I forgot to take my sleeping bag. I couldn't believe I had forgotten it, but it just wasn't there. I felt so foolish. The Indians provided me with some blankets. I was surprised they had any to spare, since they usually have only the bare necessities. It may be that some of them went without their blankets so I could stay warm.

Just as I got the Land Rover all packed and was saying good-bye to my family, Karlene (our youngest daughter), ran to me and asked me to put her on my shoulders and run around the house. I told her I didn't have time and started to back out of our drive-way. Then, I thought, "What if I never come back? What if I go over a cliff and am pinned under the car? What is the one thing I would be thinking about?" The one thing that would come to my mind was that I hadn't taken time to carry Karlene around the house on my shoulders. I was sure I'd think, "It would have just taken a small amount of time and now I am dying here and will never have a chance to carry her again." So, I pulled back into the driveway and said, "Karlene, hop on my shoulders," and I ran around the house with her and let her down. This time as I drove off I thought, "Now, I am ready to die!"

The roads to most of these villages wind up the rugged mountainside. They are all dirt and if it is ... or has been raining, the mud makes it almost impassible even with a four-wheel drive vehicle. The deep ruts and the large holes that the horses have made with their hooves, all fill with water and make stability very difficult. There is almost always only one road to a village. That means we nearly always came down the same way we went up the mountain to the village. Coming down had its own exciting set of problems in the mud—much different than going up!

An Indian believer and I arrived at this small village high in the Andes Mountains late in the afternoon. The believers were all waiting for us and we got busy setting all the equipment in place for the films and the service that night.

The small hut where the church service was to be held was packed to overflowing. When I gave the invitation at the end of the service, five Indians came forward. The Indians never close their eyes during the invitation. In fact, when someone gets up to come forward, all the rest of the Indians clap. At first I didn't particularly like that idea, but I soon learned that was their way of expressing their happiness when one of their family members or neighbors came to know Christ. So I, too, began to clap.

In another village where we had been attacked with stones and clubs some six months earlier, some of the believers' homes had been burned to the ground during the meetings. Now we were back there for more meetings. The church was packed with over two hundred Indians. Even the hostile Indians enjoyed seeing the gospel films. We were all hoping there wouldn't be any trouble this time.

The heavy fog in this high mountainous area had settled in the church building itself. The building was in the process of being built and they had not yet been able to afford to put the new roof on. So all that really existed of the church building was four walls. The fog was so dense that one could hardly see. We could feel the cold and dampness (almost rain) that came out of the impenetrable fog. Then, just as we feared, the rain began to patter around us.

We had promised these Indian people that we would bring gospel films and we wondered how we could show them under these conditions. I decided the only way to show the films was to back the car up to the front door of the church and show the films from the back of the car. About 150 Indians came to the meeting. They sat in the rain to see the films. By the time I was ready to preach, the rain tapered off to a drizzle. The people, eager to hear God's Word, remained throughout the entire service.

When I gave the invitation, several Indians came forward and everyone began to clap. If one comes forward from the very back of the church it takes quite a bit of time because they have to step over and around all the Indians and babies sitting on the dirt floor—there are no aisles. A lady got up from the very back and started making her way forward. The Indians started clapping. The closer she got to the front of the church, the louder they clapped until you could hardly hear yourself think. I thought to myself, "Why is she so important?" We had prayer with the new believers, after which one of the elders hurried up to me and said, "Do you know who that lady is?" I said, "I have no idea." Then he told me that she was the one who organized all the attacks the last time we were in that village for meetings. He was so excited and said, "Just think! Now she is one of us!"

I couldn't help but thank God for His grace. He had done a lot of work in that lady's heart to make her willing to make a public profession of her relationship to Christ. She knew that all the Indians she had influenced and taught to hate the believers would now hate **her** and do the things to **her** she had led them to do to other believers. Later that evening, she asked me to forgive her for the attack six months earlier. She said, "I just didn't understand. Now I do." We hugged and had prayer with the leadership. We were thrilled and she went away with the joy of the Lord in her heart.

I soon learned that clapping during the invitation does not hinder the working of the Holy Spirit. There were no secret raising of hands to accept Christ when the invitation was given. Every eye was open. If you accepted Christ, you had to do it publicly and that is good.

One thing that did bother me at first was the mothers' nursing their children right in the service. They had no shame because

God made them that way. Nursing was just a way to feed their babies. Many times there were six or eight mothers nursing, all at the same time. When one side went dry, they would simply let the baby feed from the other side. The problem was that they never covered up at all. When the baby finished nursing, the mother held the baby on her lap and let it sleep without covering herself at all. It was difficult to try to preach with all this going on right in the front of the crowd. But even though it bothered me at first, after a while, I never even noticed.

We had a good service and I was planning to return home after we got all packed up again. About that time, some believers came running back up the road and announced that the only exit over the rugged winding mountain road had been cut in three places and drunk Indians were waiting with clubs and machetes.

Cutting the road was a famous trick of the unsaved Indians. They dug a ditch across the road where there was an embankment on one side and a canyon on the other. This made it impossible to go around the ditch. Then they waited for us to leave. When we arrived at that point in the road, they planned to attack us with clubs and rocks. This happened to me many times and I simply waited until about three o'clock in the morning when the drunk Indians went home to sleep. Then, with the help of the Christians, we filled in the ditch and I returned home. You can imagine what Monnie was thinking when I didn't come home on or about the time I was expected. I told her, "Don't worry about me. I worry more about you worrying about me than I worry about the situation in which I find myself." So, she never worried. (Fat chance!)

Since three of the new believers expressed a desire to be baptized, I decided to spend the night. I expected the hostile Indians to give up and go home. However, the next morning, I learned that they spent all night waiting for me and now more Indians were joining the ones who were already there. They dug a ditch across the road six feet wide and four feet deep. I'd never seen anything like that before.

The Christians told me the only way out to the main road was a horse trail through the canyon. The problem with that trail was that there was no bridge over the small river at the bottom of the canyon. Even if I could get the four-wheel drive vehicle to the bottom of the canyon, I still could not get across the river unless we built a make-shift bridge on which to cross.

Baptizing in a Cold Mountain Stream

After I baptized the three believers in the cold mountain stream, we started making plans for a small bridge at the bottom of the canyon. I looked over the horse trail and figured I would be able to get the car to the bottom of the canyon. The Indians took *the doors off their houses* to lay across the long poles spanning the river. The riverbanks were about ten to fifteen feet above the water. The bridge was built from one bank to the other. That meant if the bridge did not hold, my car would fall ten to fifteen feet into the water. I definitely did not want that to happen, but I had to escape somehow. It was just a matter of time before the hostile Indians came to the church.

When the bridge was completed, I pulled the car slowly onto the bridge and realized it was not going to hold all that weight. The Indians brought in more long poles and reinforced the shaky bridge. I was very nervous about making another attempt. The Indians were always wanting to go for a ride in the car, but when I asked who wanted to ride over the bridge with me, I had no takers. They said they would watch from the banks of the river. I really couldn't blame them.

Building a Bridge to Escape

I put the car in four-wheel drive, in low gear and prayed that God would get me across the bridge. This time, I didn't pull onto the bridge slowly, but popped the clutch and gave it as much gas as

I could and still be able to stop before the car hit an embankment just on the other side of the bridge. The car lunged forward and I made it across the bridge just as it collapsed behind me.

The Christian Indians cheered for joy as this meant that I had escaped the confrontation with the enemy. After looking at the broken-down bridge for a while, I had a word of prayer with the believers, thanking the Lord for them and for His hand of deliverance for me and my car. However, I still had to get up the other side of the canyon over virtually impossible terrain. As I reached the top of the canyon and looked back, I could see about 25 hostile Indians on horseback who had arrived to harass and threaten the believers who remained on the other side of the broken-down bridge.

A few months later, I was invited back to this same village. The Indians planned a full week of Bible conference. The young church I helped to establish was going to be one year old. The few believers had undergone great persecution but they remained faithful to the Lord. They desired to reach their relatives, friends and neighbors for Christ in spite of the fact that these were the very ones who were constantly harassing them.

The Indians assured me that they had built a good, strong bridge over the river so I would have two ways out of their village. This gave me a little more peace of mind. They also widened the horse trail up and down the canyon so a vehicle could make it with very little problem.

As I arrived at the home of one of the believers, all the Christians were waiting to greet me with big smiles on their faces. They were expecting a great week of Bible teaching. There were two grass huts on the property. One was their kitchen where the food was to be prepared and served to all those attending the Bible conference. As I looked at the other hut, I noticed they had extended it with a large tarpaulin at the front, making kind of a tent-like shelter that connected with the mud hut. They had removed the entire front wall of the hut in order to make one large room with the hut and tent connected. They wanted enough room for 100 Indians to visit. They hoped their friends and neighbors would come. Straw was scattered over the dirt floor on which all who came could sit. It was a very primitive meeting place, but served very well.

I set up the power plant and ran extension cords for the projector and two 100-watt light bulbs. We hung up the white bed sheet on the wall at the front of the meeting place, and set up the projector. Now, all we needed were people, and people we had. Over 200 Indians packed into this small meeting place. They didn't seem to mind being packed in like sardines. The song service lasted more than an hour and we still were going to have the message and gospel films.

My little power plant ran for just over an hour on a tank of gas, so every hour I had to refill the tank. Just to get through all the Indians was a major problem. They were packed in there so tightly, they couldn't even move over to let me by. I tried to step over them, but sometimes I stepped on a leg or hand. I did manage not to step on the sleeping babies who were lying on the straw.

A group of more mature Christian Indians from another province came and presented a Christian drama each night. The singing, preaching, gospel films and drama made for a full service which lasted until after midnight every night. Then the Bible studies started at nine o'clock each morning and lasted all day. Many believers from other places came to participate and learn more of God's Word.

It was really a great week! Even though this area had been a stronghold of Satan, nine Indians came to know Christ as their personal Savior during the conference. This was evidence that the Lord was at work in this remote place. The fact that we had no open opposition was also a good sign. I never had to use the bridge again.

Chapter 10

His Eye Is On the Sparrow

This story was told to me by the Christian Indians: It was a beautiful clear day. The mountain air was clean and fresh. A slight breeze was blowing. It was a breathtaking scene to look over the beautiful patchwork farmland on the sides of the mountains. The majestic snow-capped Mt. Chimborazo loomed in the distance.

The Indians who had just been baptized were rushing to get out of their cold, wet clothing. There was a feeling of joy among the few believers present. They planned a feast after the baptismal service. Near the Indian hut, the air was filled with the smell of food being prepared—soup, rice, guinea pig (head and all) and many other things were being cooked over the open fire.

However, there hung over the group a preoccupation. Especially concerned was the mother of a tiny baby boy. The rumor had spread through the mountains that her son was born with horns and a tail. The Indians believed that he was born this way because the mother was a Christian. The mountain Indians, being very superstitious, said they were going to kill this baby.

Just as the group of Christians were ready to eat, they heard a trumpet on a far mountain. They rushed outside to see hundreds and hundreds of Indians coming with clubs, machetes, and rocks. The Christians knew why they were being attacked. They were coming to kill the baby boy!

Hurriedly, the mother and father of the infant ran behind the bushes and dug a hole. They placed the tiny baby in the hole, covered it with straw and prayed, "Lord, please protect our son."

For over two hours, these hostile Indians searched for the child. The baby lay quietly in the dark hole and never made a sound. Finally, it was all over. The believers were badly beaten. The food was stolen or ruined, but **the baby was saved!**

Some years later when this story was related to me, I was invited to hold meetings at the church that was subsequently built by those believers. The appointed time came and when I arrived in the area of the church, I was met by several believers who came to carry all the equipment up the mountain. I couldn't believe my eyes when they pointed out the rather large church building very high on the side of a mountain. It seemed like it was straight above us. I asked, "Do we have to walk clear up there?" The Indians laughed and said, "It is just a fifteen-minute walk." I commented, "Maybe for you!" An hour or so later, we arrived at the church.

We had wonderful meetings that weekend. Ten Indians accepted the Lord, among them a 12-year-old boy. *He was the baby that had been saved* from the savage Indians who wanted to kill him.

His story reminds me of the baby Moses and how he was saved from being killed. Perhaps, some day, this boy will be a mighty voice for God like Moses was.

* *

I thought it would be fun to take the family along on a certain one-day trip into the mountains. I didn't expect any trouble in the village where we would minister. We could have a picnic on the way and let our grandchildren, Peggy and Scott Salzman, enjoy the mountains and an Indian service. Our daughter, Shari and her husband, Paul, and Peggy and Scott would go with Monnie and me to the village nearly four hours from Quito. On the way, we had a picnic beside a small mountain stream. Peggy and Scott had a great time playing.

Then we left the main road, which is called the Pan-American Highway, and after an hour over a narrow, winding mountain dirt road, we came to the end of the road where we were to leave our vehicle. The meeting place was about a half a mile from the end of the road in the patio of the home of a Christian Indian. We were to walk that distance, but it was on level ground and not a difficult walk.

As I stopped at the end of the road, drunk Indians, men and women alike, came running up to us and surrounded the car. They were really wild and it made us all nervous. However, the believers assured us that our car would be safe where it was parked. Just to be sure, we left a Christian Indian to guard it. The drunks finally staggered off down the road. We thought it was the end of that problem.

We all made our way down the path to the Indian's home for the meeting. The Christian Indians came to carry the projector, generator and literature to the patio. There were only six Christian Indians in this area.

After setting up the equipment, as it got dark, we started the first film. There were more than 100 Indians packed into that small patio. The patio was closed on three sides with a high mud wall which connected to the front of their thatched roof home. This gave us protection from the cold mountain wind.

While the first film was being shown, Paul, my-son-in-law, and I heard shouting, whistling and a lot of commotion coming from where the car was parked.

I had asked a visiting pastor to bring the message that night. Just as the pastor was ready to preach, some Indians came rushing into the crowd shouting, "They are beating up on the people and they are destroying the missionary's car." I quickly packed up all the equipment and put it in a corner of the hut. I had an idea the drunk Indians would come to the meeting place and cause trouble. I also had Monnie, Shari, Peggy and Scott hide in the same corner and we put a table in front of them, hoping that if we were attacked the hostile Indians would not find them.

The disturbance continued down by the car, but they never made a move in our direction. I was surprised that no one left the meeting. We got the Indians quieted down and the pastor gave his message. Even though we could still hear the confusion down by the car, the Indians listened to the message and hearts were touched. Twenty-one Indians responded to the invitation to accept Christ as their personal Savior.

When someone accepts Christ under these conditions, you know they really mean business. They could hear the unsaved Indians attacking and they knew that when they left the meeting, having made a public profession of Christ, they might be clubbed, stoned, or even killed. Still they came forward.

By this time, I was told that the road was blocked with tree trunks and large rocks and that the two front tires on the car were completely flat. We prayed that they had not been slashed with a machete. The drunk Indians were waiting in the darkness with clubs, machetes and rocks to attack us when we made our way back to the car.

Since the Indians had not attacked the meeting place and none of the Indians wanted to leave, even though it was quite late, I told them I would show two more gospel films if, after that, they would help us clear off the road. They agreed and I got the equipment unpacked and showed them two more gospel films—the pastor preached to the crowd again. At midnight, Paul and I, along with some Christian Indians went to see if the way was clear for us to leave and to find out how badly the car had been damaged. The antagonistic Indians were nowhere to be found. Apparently, they got tired of waiting for us and went home to sleep off their drunkenness. So it was safe for us to leave.

We thanked the Lord the tires had not been slashed. They had only let the air out of them. Fortunately, I had an attachment that fit into a spark plug hole on the car to pump up the tires. Thank the Lord there was no other damage to the car. Once again, we experienced the protection and the blessing of God.

Many of the Indians, both saved and unsaved helped us clear off the road and by one o'clock in the morning, we were ready for the long trip home. The Christians asked me if I would come back and I assured them I would. We set a date for my return trip. We never had another problem in that area over the years and the church grew and enjoyed the blessing of God.

* *

I couldn't believe the place the Indians had prepared for me to sleep! A portion of the platform in the church had a partial wall around my bed. This would have been a very nice arrangement had the church service ended at a reasonable time, but I knew that the Indians continued singing until the wee hours of the morning and I needed a good night's sleep to be fresh for the next day's activities.

I had traveled nearly five hours through driving rain and over some roads where the four-wheel drive on my car barely kept me from sliding into the deep canyons below. When I reached a point where the trail was too steep and muddy for the car, a group of Indians were waiting for me with some pack horses and a horse for me to ride.

With the rain still pouring down, all the equipment (projector, powerplant, gasoline, amplifier, loud speaker, films, extension cords, literature, sleeping gear, etc.) was loaded and tied on the horses. For the next hour, we made our way up the steep, slippery mountain trail. In some places the horses could not even keep their footing and began to slide backwards down the mountain.

Finally, we reached the church and I wondered how many Indians would come out for the meeting in this kind of weather. The Indians began arriving at 6:30 in the evening and by 7:30 the little church that could comfortably hold 100 was packed with nearly 300 Indians. After lots of singing and a gospel film, I preached and seven Indians stepped out to receive Jesus Christ as their personal Savior.

After the second gospel film was shown, I retired to my "bedroom" on the platform. As I had surmised, another song service took place and it lasted until two o'clock in the morning. Then the Indians who had come from a long distance bedded down in the small church building. At four o'clock in the morning, we all were awakened by a radio turned up full volume to listen to HCJB's Quichua broadcast.

We had Bible studies during the day and that night even more Indians came to the meeting in spite of the rain. After my part in the evening service, I retired to my little room on the platform. I rolled up toilet tissue and put it in my ears to muffle out part of the noise. It seemed to work quite well and I was just about asleep when I heard someone calling my name, over and over. I asked what he wanted and he said, "This man wants to buy a Bible." I thought aloud, "At two o'clock in the morning?" I'd never been awakened that hour, but I got up and got him a Bible. I sure hope he read it that night!

By then, the service was over and some of the Indians kept talking through the night. The ones who were not talking, were snoring. It seemed like *every* Indian who was not talking was snoring. The Indians could sleep right through all that noise, but I couldn't. When I got home, I ordered some ear plugs from a gun shop in the States. After I began using the ear plugs, I coud sleep through amost anything.

The roads were almost always a problem. If they were not muddy and slick, they were dusty and dirty. When it rained a lot, there were always landslides. If the landslides were small, I could get around them if there was room on the side of the mountain road, but if I came upon a large slide, I might be trapped in an area for several days.

One night, I had just finished a good series of meetings in a remote village and was on my way home very late at night when I rounded a curve and there, directly before me, was a huge landslide. I knew that if I couldn't get through the landslide I was trapped in the remote Indian village.

I began digging and throwing rocks and pushing the small boulders off the road into the canyon below. I could hear the boulders crashing through the brush for what seemed like a full minute before they eventually reached the bottom. I figured the canyon floor had to be a thousand feet below. While I continued digging using my headlights for light, some Indians came on horseback from the opposite direction and informed me that the road had many mud and rock slides, but this one was the largest. It was caused by three days of torrential rains.

My concern for the moment was just to get through this landslide. I could see there was a huge boulder blocking the largest part of the road and I knew it would be absolutely impossible to move it. With the help of the Indians, I kept digging. My hope was that I could somehow squeeze by this big boulder. I got into the car and prayed, "Lord don't let this car go over the side." Then, I put the car into four-wheel drive and began to creep along the ledge around the boulder. I looked over the edge into the darkness of the canyon and I knew it must be a long way to the bottom. The Indians walked beside the car, guiding me, so I would drive as close to the boulder as possible. Finally, they informed me I had passed the boulder and was safe. I breathed a sigh of relief and thanked the Lord for His protection.

The rains were a constant problem. Even though I had rain gear, it never really kept me dry. Most of the meetings were held in semi-dry buildings. I was never fully protected from the inclement weather. I found there are a *lot* of leaky roofs in Ecuador. I have slept under my share of them and held meetings in the rest. When the meetings (in rainy weather) involved more than one day ... and most of them did, it meant constantly wearing damp clothing and sleeping in a cold, damp sleeping bag. My goose-down coat weighed a ton when it was wet. The Indians fared no better as we all sat around an open fire to eat, I in my wet coat and they in their wet ponchos.

But the rain never seemed to keep the Indians away from the meetings. Some of them walked four or five hours over the mountains to attend the meetings. They all wore knee-high rubber boots and most of them wore no socks. That way they could just dump the water out of their boots and keep going.

One night, after a meeting in an Indian village, I was awakened about three-thirty in the morning by that dreadful sound of drip, drip, drip. The horrible thought came to me that my sleeping bag was being saturated by a leak in the roof. I was right! It was soaking wet! I reached out to see in what condition my coat might be and it was even wetter than my sleeping bag. What a mess that was, but I lived through it, even though I wondered at times if I would.

One meeting we held was in a small community about 14,000 feet up in the mountains. The wind was blowing a gale. The Indians huddled together behind a large haystack in their heavy woolen ponchos for protection from the cold, strong wind. Between films, Tod and Karlene presented special music. A gospel message was given in both the Spanish and Quichua languages. In spite of the bitter cold, the Christian Indians, one after another, stood to their feet and gave their testimonies of what God was doing in their lives. Even though the meeting started at seven, we were still hearing testimonies and singing until nearly eleven. That night 17 Indians gave their hearts to the Lord Jesus Christ.

As we put away the equipment, we thought the Indians had all gone home, but we found 50 of them waiting for us in the tiny hut where we were to spend the night. They were still singing and eating boiled potatoes prepared by our host. About midnight, they all bedded down with us for the rest of the night. We had wall-to-wall people with some Indians sitting up for lack of room to stretch out.

The next morning, we were awakened at four o'clock by the radio loudly proclaiming God's Word from HCJB in the Quichua language. The Indians listen daily with great interest! After breakfast, Bible study was held and five more Indians received Christ. Things like that are what kept us going.

At another village (Cangahua), we were told that we were the first ones to come to them with the gospel. We had only recently learned that this village had never had contact with the gospel— and there were 1,000 people living there. It was a rather desolate place ...cold and windy, without much activity. You could say the place was *dead* , but worse than that, they were spiritually dead without Christ. So, we took our gospel films and went to their village.

Over 300 people turned out for this occasion and at the end of the service, there were ten adults and several children who gave their lives to Jesus. Two young couples who accepted the Lord were from another village which had no contact with the gospel, either. They invited us to visit their village, too! We either had to go to them with our films and music and messages, or we had to tell them, "No", and we couldn't do that.

Over Two Thousand Indians in One Tent

Chapter 11

Expect the Unexpected

I never knew what to expect when I was invited into a new area. Sometimes the communities had no church buildings and the meetings were held in tents, out in the open air, in individual homes, beside haystacks or in a cornfield.

Sometimes the trip was twelve to fourteen hours by car each way. Other times, it was just a few hours by car. Sometimes I could drive right up to the place where the meeting was going to be held and other times we had to walk for hours over trails of deep, sticky mud and often, I went in on horseback.

That is what made it so exciting. I never knew what I would find at the end of the road. Sometimes the Indians were friendly and sometimes they were hostile. But there was one thing of which I was always certain—God would always bless His Word and, if I had the opportunity to preach the gospel, there were always decisions for Christ—sometimes there were few and sometimes there were many. Monnie never asked me "if" we saw decisions. She always asked me "how many" decisions there were. Sometimes, the response was not great in number, but *it was always significant.* God was doing a great work among the highland Indians of Ecuador. They are precious people and God revealed His love for them abundantly.

At one point, my entire staff at the Print Shop and I were working closely with the missionaries of the Gospel Missionary Union to produce a most attractive, 270-page, illustrated Old Testament storybook in the Quichua language. When it was ready, it was decided this occasion was so important that we would hold a dedication of the book and offer them for sale for the first time to the Quichua Indians at Colta, an Andean village at 14,000 foot elevation where the Gospel Missionary Union has worked for many years.

When I arrived at Colta, I found that the Christians had rented a tent in which to have their services. The Indians came by foot, horseback, busload, bicycle and even by train until nearly 3,000 had gathered. The three-hour service was a beautiful sight to behold as these thousands of Indians, clad in their colorful native dress (many of them barefooted and hundreds of women with babies strapped to their backs) stood on their feet during the entire service. They listened to several different speakers and to special music. Part of the program consisted of music and drama by various children's groups.

Bible Conference in a Large Tent

When they held the new books in their hands, it was thrilling to watch them page through and talk excitedly in their native language about the dozens of colored pictures they found there. Watching them, we realized anew the importance of Christian literature. The Gospel Missionary Union was teaching them to read in the school there. Now, the Indians held in their hands God's written truth. We knew, because of what God's Word means to us, that they would be blessed as they thought about the Bible stories and made them a vital part of their lives.

These believers had undergone severe persecution from their neighbors, but they still had a deep desire to see their people accept Jesus Christ as personal Savior. That week, God honored their faith in a wonderful way as 95 of these Quichuas stepped out to accept Jesus Christ as their personal Savior during the four-day conference.

The first night I preached, 25 Indians came forward to accept Christ. They were standing on an elevated platform and it collapsed! No one was hurt, but the next day, the Indians reinforced the platform. That night after the message, 40 Indians came forward to accept Christ and the platform collapsed again! Again, there were no injuries. The next day, a different type of platform was constructed and it didn't collapse again.

During those four days, we had Bible studies each day. I had the privilege of baptizing fourteen Indians and performing a Christian marriage. We also had a wonderful time around the Lord's table.

A week of hard work had come to an end, but it was very gratifying work. As we left that mountain lake and the villages surrounding it, the wind was still blowing up a gale and the dust was thick. The place was very dirty, but thank God, there were many whose hearts were cleansed by the blood of Jesus Christ. Each week, we returned home to our regular schedules of school, work in the print shop, cooking and cleaning, but our hearts were thrilled with seeing God at work.

* * * * * * * * * * * * * * * * * * *

The Lord does, indeed, work in mysterious ways. One day while I was busy working in the print shop, I was approached by one of our HCJB medical doctors, Ron Guderian. He asked if I would like to go on a medical caravan into the northern jungle of Ecuador. They needed an evangelist to accompany the three doctors on this trip. This would mean over a week away from my responsibilities at the print shop. Since I was Director of the Print Shop, I would have to line up all the work ahead of time (thank the Lord for excellent helpers) and get permission from our Field Director to go. I told them I would love to go with them if I could arrange everything.

I received permission to go, lined up all the work at the print shop and prepared all I would need for the trip. The missionary in the jungle, Les Meisenheimer, had a projector and power plant but I took along my own gospel films.

We left Quito on a bus that took us to the coast. We spent the first night at another missionary's home. The next morning, bright and early, we boarded a barge and went up the coastline. This barge was the only way the coastal people went from town to town. As a result, it was packed with all kinds of things. The people carried chickens, pigs, sheep, goats, and cows as well as all their produce for the different markets along the way. To say the least, it was not a luxury liner. There is no way to explain the heat and the various smells—you had to be there! Just use your imagination! After traveling a full day on the barge, we arrived at a small village where Les met us. We spent the night in this coastal village of Limones. Limones is a hot, humid, foul-smelling place. Even the Ecuadorians agree to this.

There are sawmills in this village and all the sawdust is thrown on the ground and spread out. Boardwalks are built on top of the sawdust. This would not be so bad if it weren't for the oceantide that comes up and soaks the sawdust under the streets and boardwalks. Then the tide goes out. The hot coastal sun comes out, causing the wet sawdust to sour, giving off a really sickening smell.

Early the next morning, we climbed into a dug-out canoe that took us up the river to the mission station deep in the northern jungles of Ecuador. As we made our way up the river, Les told me, "We haven't had a single conversion in my village in the last two years. It just seems that God has taken His hand of blessing off this place. We've had youth meetings, special meetings and other types of meetings and nothing has happened." What a challenge that was to me! I was accustomed to seeing souls saved in every meeting among the Quichua Indians. I wondered how I was going to respond to this lack of interest.

When we arrived at the mission station (called Zapallo Grande), all the Indians came running down to the riverbank to welcome us. These were Cayapa Indians and completely different from the Quichuas. The men wore pants and shirts, but the women wore only a skirt.

One of the Indians called out, "Which one of you is the dentist?"

"We didn't bring a dentist," replied one of the doctors. "We are all medical doctors."

"Don't say that!" the Indian said. "You must have brought a dentist because we have so many people here with bad teeth."

All three doctors looked at me and I shook my head very emphatically and said, "No way! The only teeth I've ever pulled are my kids' baby teeth."

One of the doctors then said to me, "Oh, there's nothing to it!" And that seemed to settle the question.

I ended up pulling 73 teeth that week. The tools were there and I used them, but it was the Lord who was working.

I was surprised to see an Indian man, Carlos, whom I had met a few years earlier. Carlos had taken me up river in his dug-out canoe to look at some large pipe left there by the Germans. They had a large gold mining camp in the jungle before World War II. The large pipe was still there and the HCJB engineers thought it might be used for our dam at Loreto, but it turned out that we couldn't use it.

Carlos was a skilled navigator on the river and I witnessed that firsthand. While we were deep in the jungle, the river started rising. There are times when you don't expect the river to rise because it is a beautiful day in the jungle. However, the rains in the distant mountains cause the jungle river to rise. It can rise from ten to twenty feet in a very short time. When it does, the river is nearly impossible to navigate. Large logs and entire trees come crashing down the river as it rises.

This particular day, while we were on the river, it started rising and we had no place to escape its fury. We would have both been killed had it not been for the skill of Carlos as he maneuvered the dug-out canoe. We became very close friends on that trip.

The missionary told me that Carlos was no longer walking with the Lord, but that he wanted to help me pull teeth. I agreed and we were to be open "for practice" on Monday morning. Practicing medicine has a whole new meaning to me now, as that was what I was doing, "practicing" my dental skills with God's help. I got to be pretty good at it, too!

One man had a big, very bad molar that just wouldn't come out, so Carlos held his head and I stood on a chair in front of him and pulled and twisted while the man moaned and groaned. I asked him, "Shall we give up?" but he had so much pain from the decaying molar, he told us to go ahead and pull it. He said he would rather suffer the pain now, all at once, than suffer every night for weeks. We finally got the tooth out. It had three large roots that curved inward—that is why it was so hard to pull. When it came out, there was a lot of the gums that came with it.

During all this, I was reminded of another meeting, at yet another village, when one night as my daughter, Karlene, and I slept in an Indian hut, we heard an Indian lady crying in pain all night from a toothache. Here is what Karlene wrote about that trip:

"It was a new experience for me, a 15-year-old girl, to be starting out on my first overnight evangelistic trip with my father. The trip proved to be very exciting. After we left the main road, we travelled up a 'kind of a road' that had a river running right down the middle of it. As we went on up the road, we came to a big river that crossed the road. We had to get out of the jeep to see if the road was passable. We were able to cross the river with the four-wheel drive, and as we went across, we hit a big bump and everything in the car went flying.

"Much later, high in the Andes Mountains, we reached our destination—a tiny Indian settlement. We talked with some Indian believers about where we should have the meeting. They decided the best location would be up beside the old schoolhouse. As they were taking to us, the question entered my mind as to where the road was that led to the schoolhouse. They finally gave us directions and, to my surprise, there was no road! First, they led us across a little, tiny, narrow, shaky bridge, and I wondered if it would hold up the jeep. Then, they told us the way to go would be straight up the side of a mountain through plowed fields. At one point, our jeep was leaning to the side and I was afraid it would turn over. We finally reached the schoolhouse, and that night, we showed two Gospel films and gave a Bible message. Several

Indian believers gave their testimonies about their past life and the wonderful life Jesus Christ had given them.

"After the meeting, we were shown our sleeping quarters for that night at a nearby hut. As we entered the smoke-filled hut, a mother and her children were seated around an open fire where they were preparing food. The only source of light was a tiny candle. We were told we would be sleeping on the straw that covered the cold, dirt floor. We sat down on the soft straw and we were served hot cinnamon water, bread, hard-boiled eggs and *habas*. We sang Quichua hymns around the fire. Then the family laid out their ponchos and we stretched out our sleeping bags to go to sleep. The mother spent most of the night crying because of a bad toothache."

The next morning, the Indians took heads of matches and stuffed them in the decayed part of her tooth. It seemed to help. Much later, I told my dentist in the States about the incident and he explained that the matchheads probably kept the cold air from reaching the open nerve which seemed to help her. Dentistry in the jungle is really primitive, but God uses common sense in all things.

Now, here I was in the jungle again, but this time, I was doing the work of a dentist! On Sunday morning, I preached. Even though the church was full, no one responded. That night, we had the same experience. On Monday morning when the clinic opened, I started talking to Carlos, intending to finally bring up the subject of his spiritual condition.

"Why do you suppose God is not working in this place?" I asked.

Carlos shrugged his big shoulders and answered, "I don't know."

Then I asked, "Do you think it could be because of sin in the camp?"

"Probably," the Indian answered.

"Are you walking with the Lord?" I asked.

"No," was the answer.

"Do you think maybe it's **your** sin that is hindering the work of the Holy Spirit?" I said.

"Maybe," replied Carlos.

We went on pulling teeth. Finally I asked him, "Would you like to get your life straightened out with the Lord?"

And Carlos answered, "Yes."

I told him, "I'll tell you what. Tonight after I preach and give the invitation, you come forward and confess your sins and get your life straightened out."

"Okay," said Carlos. And he seemed to be really sincere, but that night at the meeting, he didn't even show up, so the next day, I talked to him again and Carlos told me, "Tonight, I'll come."

And that night he did come. After the message, he came forward, turned to the congregation and told them that he had sinned. He said he went out and bought a revolver and was planning to kill his wife, their ten children, Les, the missionary, and himself.

"I know it was of Satan," he wept, "and I want all of you to forgive me."

Les went to him and they hugged each other. Then more people came forward and confessed that they, too, hadn't been walking with the Lord. Before the week was over, 32 Indians accepted Jesus Christ as their personal Savior. I knew that the reason I had to pull all those teeth was to have time to talk with Carlos. Les later told me that 31 of the Indians followed the Lord in baptism.

* *

On a cold, rainy night Jose Naula (HCJB's radio pastor to the Quichua Indians from the tiny radio station at Colta), another Indian and I arrived at the end of a slick, muddy mountain trail. Before us lay a little settlement situated at about 13,000 feet up in the Andes Mountains. The small Indian hut where we were to have the meeting was off the road about a mile. Jose told me to stay in the car because the Indians in this area were not very friendly.

Just after Jose left for the meeting, a large group of Indians came up to the car and started asking me why we were there and what right we had to travel that road. They seemed to be getting pretty upset and mean. They kept asking me if I had a permit to travel that road. I had no idea what they were talking about so I took out my wallet and showed them my HCJB identification card. They took it and looked at it with great interest. Since they could not read, they thought it was a permit to travel that road—which we didn't even need. When I asked them to return my card, they all took off running down the road with my card in hand. They thought they had something really important!

Hoping all was safe, I locked the car and went to the meeting place. Because of the opposition to the gospel only a few Indians attended the meeting which we held in the small Indian hut, but six of these Indians accepted the Lord as their personal Savior that night. Jose and I slept at the home of an Indian named Segundo that night. Because there was not enough room in the tiny hut, we slept outside with the goats in a lean-to beside Segundo's house. We returned to Quito the next morning.

These six believers began to grow through listening to HCJB's Quichua radio programs and reading God's Word, and they were able to lead many family members and friends to accept Christ.

By this time the Indian believers were really undergoing persecution. Their homes were burned down, their animals were killed and their crops were destroyed. In spite of that, the church continued to grow. In the press of other ministry, I hadn't thought of this little settlement for a while when Jose came into the print shop one day and told me that these believers wanted me to come out and baptize all who had accepted Christ. They remembered that we were the first ones to enter that area and they wanted us to come back and have a baptismal service and observe the Lord's Supper.

This time I took Monnie, Karlene, Tod, Shari and her husband Paul along as we were going out just for the day. The trip took just over three hours each way. Jose, another missionary and some of Jose's friends went in another car. When we arrived at the settlement, I was surprised to see armed policemen standing around the area. The Christian Indians had asked for police protection during the services. Since there is freedom of religion in Ecuador, they were able to get these policemen to protect us. The unsaved Indians were every place we looked, but they knew better than to cause problems at that point.

It was a breath-taking scene in the late afternoon, even as the cool, crisp mountain air chilled us. In the distance, figures of the Indian women were silhouetted against the majestic, snow-capped mountains as they wended their way home from the harvest fields with heavy loads of fresh-cut grain piled high on their backs. One could hardly believe these short, stocky people could carry such huge bundles of grain much larger than they were.

Watching them, our thoughts turned to the Scripture which says, *"Come unto me all ye that labor and are heavyladen, and I will give you rest"* (Matthew 11:28). The heavy loads of grain were bad enough, but their sins were even heavier to bear unless we could tell them about Jesus who wanted to be their Savior and who offered them eternal life.

We wound our way down the narrow path, bordered on both sides by mud walls which separate each person's property from his neighbor's. We were going to the home of one whose burdens had recently been lifted by the grace of God. It is the custom among the believers in this village, to welcome the new believer into the congregation by having a singspiration in his home.

As we sat with our backs nestled against the warm straw in front of the mud hut, we watched the believers come from the village and join us in a circle. Latecomers were required to sing a special number. During the service, we were all asked to quote a verse from Scripture by memory.

It was beautiful to look into the faces of the older men and women and to know that from childhood they had carried heavy burdens of fear, suspicion and guilt. Now, we could see in these dark, wrinkled faces the joy and peace that only Christ can give to any of us.

The Indians dug a hole in the ground about four feet wide and six feet long and about four feet deep. They then filled it with water from a stream. That was to be our baptismal tank. The stream ran beside the hole and they made a little ditch so some of the water from the stream was diverted into the hole in the ground. I learned after we arrived that there were 63 Indians to be baptized in that icy cold water. I knew I would be there a long time.

After ten or fifteen baptisms, the water started getting really muddy. The women put wool scarves over their heads to keep the mud out of their hair. By the time the last Indian was baptized, they were really getting a mud bath. When I tried to get out of the muddy water I realized my legs were numb and I could hardly walk to go change my clothes. After the baptism, we all returned to Segundo's home for a large Indian feast.

A year later, I returned to this settlement to find they had built a nice large church building and that the Christians now numbered around 120. There were 40 who wanted to be baptized but this time the baptism took place next to the church in clean water.

Baptizing in a Mud Pit

On Saturday night, the church was packed with nearly 400 Indians to see the gospel films and to hear God's word. As I observed the Indians partaking of the elements of the Lord's Supper, my mind went back to that open field where we first broke bread together and thanked the Lord for the way in which He had worked among these people and changed their lives through His Holy Spirit.

I continued to work with Segundo and his church. Together we went into many areas around their region and saw eleven other churches established. We faced many hardships together through the years. But much more importantly, we also shared in many blessings and victories.

Don Preaching Just Before the Communion Service

At one conference in Segundo's church, I spoke on giving and how God wanted to bless the giver. It took me a long time to realize that we, as missionaries, were doing the national church a great disservice when we provide all that a church needs in a material way. We are robbing the believers of a blessing. God wants to bless them when they are faithful in giving to the Lord, but if there are no needs, the people will not give and therefore, will not be blessed. We had a full week of Bible study on giving.

Two weeks later, Monnie and I went back to the church unannounced. We were surprised to see the offering plate piled high with bills. As if that weren't enough, after the offering plates were passed, the Indians marched to the front of the church and put money into a box. After the service, I asked Segundo what the box was for. He told me, "Oh, that is the *tithe!* What they collected in the plates was the *offering!*" We went away thanking God for the faithfulness of these believers and their desire to serve Him, as they grew in the Word.

As more years passed, we saw a great change in Segundo. An organization from the U.S. moved into Ecuador to "help" struggling churches. What we saw was just the opposite. This organization hired Segundo and other pastors to find needy churches and determine how the organization could help them. Segundo got his eyes off what God could do for the Indian churches and got his eyes on what the American organization could do for the churches.

One church would get money for a building and the believers would quit giving. The other churches then tried to get money from the organization and when they couldn't, they were resentful against the church that did. Pastors became jealous of one another. No one trusted Segundo any longer because they said he had "sold out" to the U. S. organization. It truly was a sad thing to see. Segundo left his church and went full-time with the U. S. organization and he no longer has any spiritual influence on the believers. Some Indians still like him—if they can get some financial help through him. This U. S. organization (without knowing it and in the name of "helping") is destroying the churches and robbing the believers of God's blessing. The churches need help in spiritual matters and in Christian education. They do not need what the U. S. dollar can do for them materially. My heart is greatly saddened to see this from well-meaning people who just do not understand. Nor do they want to understand the damage they are doing to the national church.

A national pastor should be paid by his people and his church building should be built by its members. If it's done any other way, someone is sure to get hurt, spiritually speaking. I've seen it too often to feel otherwise.

* * * * * * * * * * * * * * * * * * * *

The alarm announced that it was a little after four o'clock in the morning and it was time to load the four-wheel drive vehicle with all we needed for the long, hard trip deep into the north-eastern jungles of Ecuador. I was accompanied on this trip by another HCJB missionary, Byron McGuire.

The Texaco Oil Company had just built a road all the way into the jungle to a place called Lago Agrio which was a 12-hour drive from Quito. The road was built by Texaco for access through the jungle so an oil pipeline could be built from the jungles of Ecuador over the high mountains, and all the way to the coast. They needed this to remove the oil which had been discovered in that area.

After about 30 minutes of driving, we left the paved road to follow a cobblestone road up over the Continental Divide at an elevation of about 14,000 feet. As we passed HCJB's hydro-electric plant in Papallacta, we began a rapid descent over the newly-constructed road into regions unknown to us. The dirt road seemed so good at first that we wondered if we would need to use four-wheel drive. It wasn't long, however, until we were thankful that the Lord had provided us with this rugged vehicle for this very purpose.

Even though our final destination was deep in the jungle over the new road which had just opened up to the public, we paused long enough in each newly accessible little jungle village to distribute tracts and witness to the people. It was a real joy to see how receptive the people were to the gospel and to learn that nearly all of them had listened to HCJB for many years. At the same time, it saddened us to hear that no missionary had ever conducted services in these villages.

After more than 12 hours of driving, we finally reached our destination, only a few miles from the Colombian border, at the village of Lago Agrio. This village was a boomtown because of the oil companies who were working close by. Up to this time, all the men and supplies had been flown in to Lago Agrio. We were the first missionaries to enter by car. We wanted to see what opportunities there were in this area for starting churches.

As we bathed in the Agua Rico river nearby, we were captivated by the beautiful sunset reflecting on the rippling water. The Indian campfires along the river bank reminded us that night was approaching and it was time to prepare for the open air evangelistic service.

We announced over our loudspeakers mounted on the Land Rover, that we would be showing gospel films and a large crowd of about 300 people gathered for the service. They began arriving before six o'clock. Indians and homesteaders came on foot through the dense jungle from many miles around, while some caught rides on oil company trucks that were passing through on the jungle road, and others came in their own vehicles packed to the hilt with people.

Showing Gospel Films in the Jungle Village

By eight o'clock that evening, the majority of the people had arrived. What a blessing to see Quichua and Cofan Indians and Spanish settlers all gathered together, singing and praising the Lord.

After showing the first gospel film on the Birth of Christ, I gave a short message and we gave the people an opportunity to purchase New Testaments before the second film. To our delight, all the New Testaments were sold within a few minutes. After the second film on the Miracles of Christ, I gave an invitation for them to accept Christ as their Savior. There were over 40 who responded. These people were counselled by Byron and me and tracts were given to all who were at the service.

Later that night, as the torrential jungle rains poured down, we were thankful for a roof over our heads even though there were no walls except for the jungle vegetation. At dawn, we were awakened by the call of the wildlife in the jungle and we began our journey back to Quito with hearts full of joy and gratitude to the Lord.

* *

Shortly after our first trip to Lago Agrio, I talked to Carlos Jarrin about accompanying me for a five-day return trip to that area. I had seen firsthand that it was really a needy place. As in any frontier town, sin ran rampant. All the oil men had plenty of money and that brought in all the elements of sin. There was no gospel witness in the entire area.

As we made our way down the sometimes dusty, sometimes muddy narrow winding jungle road, we passed many landslides that had just been cleared. We were thankful not to be held up by the landslides. We were following the old Amazon trail which leads from Quito to the mighty Amazon River.

During that week, we were able to show gospel films in some of the oil camps. These camps housed up to 500 men. Many of them were Quichua Indians who had gone to the jungle for work in the oil fields and on the roads. The camp director asked us not to give an invitation for salvation in the dining hall where the films were shown, but we were allowed to talk to the men outside. We sold hundreds of New Testaments and some expressed a desire to accept Christ.

A military base had already been set up in this same area. One night, we were invited to show a gospel film to 600 military men. The officer in charge had all the soldiers march onto the parade ground to see the film. We showed the film from the top of our Land Rover. We had their full attention except for a few moments when some other soldiers came by, carrying a live alligator.

The first night, we drove just out of town and set up our tent on the side of the Agua Rico river. After we heated up some soup on a small, gas camp stove for our evening meal, we bedded down. Just after midnight, we were awakened from our sleep as we heard a strange noise outside our tent. With our flashlights in hand, we crawled out to see water running right next to our tent. It was really frightening to see the raging river which threatened to wipe out our camp and wash away the Land Rover. We hurriedly grabbed everything and threw it into the Land Rover and drove for higher ground. The next morning, we were told the river had risen twelve feet overnight. We could have lost our camp, our car and possibly our lives, if God hadn't awakened us in time to get away from the raging waters.

Each day, we went from house to house passing out tracts and talking to people about the Lord. We were invited into many homes for coffee or something to eat. The people in the jungle eat differently than those in the mountains. The jungle people eat lots of fried bananas and yucca. Yucca is a large stringy root that is grown in the jungle and looks much like an oblong potato. There are many ways to prepare yucca. Sometimes it is cut into thin slices like potato chips, then fried and sprinkled with salt. They are delicious. They also serve lots of fish and chicken.

In an Indian village, the Indians get drunk on a yucca drink. The women cook the yucca until it can be chewed, then they chew it until it is the consistency of mashed potatoes. They spit it out into an earthen bowl, add some water, cover it, and bury it in the ground. The saliva from the chewing of the yucca causes it to ferment. After a few weeks, the Indians drink the liquid (which is called *chicha*) and get dead drunk. I have been offered *chicha* many times, but I always politely refuse.

One thing to be said about the jungle Indians is that they are very clean. Because of the heat, they spend a lot of time bathing in the river.

Once while I was hunting in the jungle with some jungle Indians, we were chasing some monkeys. One of the monkeys, jumping from one tree to another, fell to the ground right in front of an Indian. He grabbed a club and killed the monkey. That evening the Indians built a small platform out of green tree limbs. They built a large fire under the platform and placed the monkey on top of the platform—hide, head, feet and all. The monkey cooked all night and when we arose the next morning, we saw a monkey with all his hair burned off and black as charcoal. The meat was completely cooked, but it still looked like a monkey sitting there.

The Indian cut off a piece of the monkey and gave it to me. I started to eat the monkey meat and it tasted just fine until I began to think about those little hands and those eyes looking at me. The meat I was chewing kept getting bigger and bigger and I just couldn't swallow it. I finally had to spit it out. Had I not known I was eating monkey meat, I am sure it would have been delicious.

Chapter 12

Seeds in the Wind

I made many trips into the jungle to help struggling churches. I started some of the jungle churches and others were started by the mountain Quichua Indians. The Quichuas originally went down to the jungle because the Ecuadorian government was giving away land in the jungle to encourage distribution of the population and development of new lands.

They took their faith with them and started little churches throughout the jungle. It was at one of these churches that Jose Naula and I were to have a week of meetings and dedicate a new church building. These Indians were deeper in the jungle than Lago Agrio. We passed through Lago Agrio on our way to the edge of the Napo River still four or five hours deeper into the jungle. The oil company had just finished this narrow road to the river's edge. We held the typical service as in all villages which included films, preaching, Bible studies, baptismals, weddings, baby dedications, the Lord's Supper and at this church, we were also to hold a dedication of the new church building.

We had a wonderful week of meetings in spite of the jungle rains—at least it wasn't cold. On our way home, I experienced something I had never experienced before. Not far from the village we had a flat tire. We stopped and put on the spare. When we arrived in Lago Agrio I had the flat tire fixed and purchased another used tire and rim, just in case we had more tire trouble.

We hadn't gone down the road from Lago Agrio very far when we had another flat tire. We had two spares, so we changed the tire and kept going. Not long after that flat tire, another tire went flat and I knew we needed to get the two flat tires fixed, so I sent Jose back to Lago Agrio on a truck that we hailed down, to get the tires fixed. I waited for him on the side of the road. Jose returned just as the sun was going down in the Ecuadorian jungle. We hadn't eaten since we left at seven o'clock that morning. We continued on down the rough jungle road for another two hours. Then, we heard a bump! Unbelievable! Now all four of the original tires had gone flat at one time or another.

I again sent Jose back to Lago Agrio to have two more tires fixed. When he returned, we prayed that the old tires would last ... but the Lord had other plans and soon we heard a big bang. Another tire had gone out. We still had four good tires and so we got going again as soon as that tire was changed. We were now starting up into the mountains and the air was getting cold. At about one o'clock in the morning, a dreaded hissing sound was heard and the car started weaving all over the road. There was no place to fix or to buy a tire at this hour, so all we could do was wait until morning.

About three o'clock in the morning, a bus came along and I sent Jose to Quito with two of the bad tires and a note to Monnie which read, "Buy two tires and have them sent out to me by bus - or maybe someone could bring them out to me." I waited until early afternoon. Then I saw Enoch Sanford in his Land Rover coming down the road toward me. I was really happy to see him, but to our dismay, the tires he brought would not fit my car. The mechanic at HCJB purchased the wrong size tires.

I locked up the Land Rover and both Enoch and I went back to Quito to pick up some tires and come back. It was ten o'clock at night when we finally got the tires changed and I was on the road again. Then something even more unbelievable happened. You guessed it! I had another flat tire, making a total of seven flat tires. Enoch jokingly told me, "If you have one more flat tire, I am just going to go around you and go on home." **Forty hours** after I left the jungle church, I arrived back in Quito. I was tired, dirty and hungry. In spite of the difficulties I encountered, I praised the Lord for the 32 souls that were saved and for the 12 Indians who had been baptized in the swift jungle river.

I still don't know why we had so many flat tires. Someone told me the Lord was trying to teach me patience and I replied, "Well, He didn't make the grade that time!"

* *

It was almost like an oasis in the desert to see the bright red roof of the new church as we moved up the winding dusty mountain road. The rugged countryside was beautiful with the golden grain swaying in the breeze. Indians with hand sickles were speedily cutting and stacking the wheat in large bundles while others trudged off down the mountain to their homes with huge loads on their backs. The beautiful patchwork fields were a sight to behold. Above all, the majestic, snow-capped mountain of Chimborazo loomed as a giant hovering over the thousands of Indians that live within its shadows. It was to these Indians that we had come to minister.

This particular group of Quichua believers was completely surrounded by Indians hostile to the gospel. Earlier, they had suffered severe persecution and we wondered if they would survive. Now, my youngest son, Tod (who was 14 at the time), and I were going for the dedication of the new large church building. Here is the way Tod told about that trip:

"It was late afternoon when we arrived in the small mountain village where we picked up **two armed soldiers** for protection. (Recently nearly 230 Indians had attacked the believers with clubs and machetes.) Then we started out over the bumpy, narrow, gully-washed mountain road. When we got to the end of the road, we had to travel some distance across open fields. Near the believer's home, the Indians had cut a very narrow road along the steep mountainside. Since it was dark, Dad could not see how dangerous it really was, but once we entered the road, we discovered that it was too narrow for our car. We couldn't go on, and we couldn't turn around. Many believers had gathered for the meeting and seeing our predicament, they came running with picks and shovels to widen the road. As I watched the men work by the headlights of the car, I was impressed that these people were so eager to hear the Word of God that they were willing to chop a road through to the site of their new church.

"We quickly unloaded the projector and small portable power plant and started the service. Dad preached between the films, and when he gave the invitation, five people accepted the Lord. After the second film, opportunity was given for the Indians to give their testimony. One after another stepped forward to testify of what Christ had done for them and how He had changed their life. At midnight, we were just closing the service when an Indian lady asked if it was too late for her to accept Christ. We had prayer with her and and a couple more Indians gave their testimony before we went to the Indian hut to sleep.

"As usual, we were awakened at 4:00 in the morning with the radio blaring out the Quichua gospel program from HCJB. The Sunday morning service began about 9:00 and after lots of singing and a Bible study, several children were dedicated to the Lord. Then Dad brought a message to dedicate the new church building which the Indians had built. He challenged them to confess their sins before the dedication of the church, and I was surprised to see how the Holy Spirit worked in the hearts of these primitive Indians, because for more than an hour and a half, these people poured out their hearts to the Lord, getting right with one another and with God. Then a circle was formed and a dedicatory prayer was given in both Spanish and in Quichua. To my surprise, an Indian couple stepped into the middle of the circle and asked Dad if they could accept the Lord."

When we arrived, the believers came running out to meet us with smiling faces. What a joy it is to share the Word of God with people who are so eager to hear! The evening service lasted until four A.M. the night before and at that hour, we were served hot cinnamon water, hard-boiled eggs and bread as the service continued with more singing and testimonies. The service lasted all night long.

At daybreak, we left the church to go to the river for a baptismal service. Much to our dismay, Tod and I learned that the river was at the bottom of a deep canyon, the sides of which were nearly straight up and down, a walking distance of three miles. We wondered if our weary bodies could make the long trip down, let alone the strenuous trip back up the steep walls of the canyon, but God enabled and that morning, 24 Indians were baptized.

Upon our return to the church, colorful ribbons had been placed in the entrance of the building for the dedication of the church. After my message and a prayer of dedication outside of the building, we cut the ribbons and people entered the church for the communion service which brought the 18-hour church service to a close.

Exhausted from loss of sleep, Tod and I left for more meetings that were to be held in another village. That night, approximately 500 Quichua Indians gathered to watch the gospel films. Jose Naula preached and six Indians accepted Christ. Others jeered, blaming the Christians for the lack of rain in this particular area for nearly two years. Jose closed in prayer, asking the Lord to send rain ... and He did! At six o'clock the next morning, it began to rain. After the church service that morning (which included two weddings in which I officiated), it was still raining. And it was **still raining** when we left the village that afternoon. We thanked God that He answered this prayer in such a wonderful way. Perhaps this testimony of the Lord's faithfulness would reach into the hearts of the many Indians in that area who needed Him.

I returned to this village six months later for a four-day Bible conference. The believers had been threatened by the unsaved Indians and told that 15 communities were coming together to disrupt the conference and to set up roadblocks so that no one could come in or leave the village.

On the first day of the conference, homes of two believers were burned to the ground. By the third day, the Indian believers were becoming more and more apprehensive. They wondered if and when these threats would be carried out to the fullest. Now, more than half of the 300 believers abandoned the meetings. I inquired as to why everyone was leaving. I was informed that another believer's home was being burned and that these Indians were all going home to protect their property. Needless to say, the message that night had no effect as even those who remained were wondering what was happening in the community.

I praise God that in spite of this type of persecution, 18 Indians stepped out to accept Christ as their personal Savior during this four-day conference. On the last day, it was a beautiful sight to see all the believers gather at the river to witness the baptism of 16 Indians and to return to the church to partake of the Lord's Supper.

Every six months, I traveled to this same village for a Bible conference. The next time I went, I learned that a different believer had to pay for all the food each time a conference was held. Sometimes it put them in debt for years. They explained that this was the way it used to be done when they celebrated their saint's day, before they were saved. I told them they should **all** share the burden and that way they could **all** receive a blessing. They told me that they were all were poor people and couldn't give to the Lord. I decided it was time to have some classes on giving!

I started by telling them they looked pretty healthy and it appeared they had enough to eat. They said, "Yes, but there is nothing left over." I asked them if they knew why. They told me, "No." I explained to them that they were robbing God. "Would you help someone who is robbing you?" I asked. They said, "No, but we are poor." I pressed on and asked them how many bites of food they consumed each day. Some of them said 100 and others said 1,000. So we settled on 200. I then said to them,"You eat 200 bites of food every day, how many of those bites belong to God?" They knew that at least ten percent belonged to God and they responded, "20 bites." I asked them if they gave Him that. They said, "We can't give Him our food!" "Oh, yes you can," I answered, "One out of very ten sacks of potatoes belongs to God and one out of ten cows belongs to God." I went on at length.

Then I asked them, "What if I came to your house and you had just ten potatoes and that is all you had. Suppose you cooked them and we sat down to eat, how many of the potatoes would you give me as your guest?" Most them said, "I would give you five." Some of them probably stretched the truth and said, "I would give you six or more," but none of them said they would give me less than five potatoes. Then I asked, "How many of those potatoes does God ask of you? He only asks for *one*, but you take **all ten** of them and **maybe** cut off a very small sliver and give it to God! It is no wonder God does not bless you!" That was just part of the lessons during the week.

Six months later when we returned for the next conference, the Indians were really excited and they said, "Come, brother Don and see what we have done!" To my surprise, they had built a two-story building beside the church where they could bring visitors to sleep.

At the back, they had a large place to prepare food. They took me to the front of the building to a locked door. They opened the door and the room was filled with all kinds of food that **each family** brought for the conference. Seeing how excited they were about the blessing of giving, it made me ashamed of my own lack of giving. God was truly blessing them.

The service that evening was more than packed out with over 200 Indians in attendance. Nearly half of these were believers from other villages. The others were unsaved neighbors who watched the gospel films with great interest and who listened intently as the message was preached. However, their hearts were like stone. In the three nights we were there, only three Indians accept the Lord.

But we were thrilled with the response of the believers in the Bible studies when Don taught on the Christian family during the day. The interest was exceptional and many expressed that these studies are what was really needed in the churches.

In time, this church became a shining light in that area. They helped to start many other churches and had three teams out every weekend, preaching and teaching. When Monnie and I left Ecuador, we left our projector, power plant and most of the gospel films with these dear Indians.

* * * * * * * * * * * * * * * * * * * *

Her front teeth had been knocked out and blood was gushing from her mouth as she shouted accusations at us. The now toothless Indian lady had accused an Indian man of being a Christian and in his anger, he knocked out all her front teeth.

This Indian settlement was nearly 14,000 feet high in the mountains and had never received a gospel team before. In fact, they even refused to let the government census takers into the village the prior year. My first clue that there was a problem came when a mob of people charged toward my vehicle as I drove into the village. They were shouting, "If anyone gets killed, it will be your fault!"

Since the Indians were fighting among themselves because of my presence, I retreated to a nearby hill to show the gospel films and to preach to more than 200 of those who were interested. After the service which ended about 9:30 in the evening, I was asked to show the films in a run-down school house in the middle of a valley. I was assured that the troublemakers had gone home; however in the middle of the film, they returned, shouting and causing a great disturbance. I continued the service until almost midnight and when I gave the invitation 50 Indians accepted the Lord.

As I prepared to leave, several Indians informed me that the road was blocked in three different places and that hostile Indians were waiting for me with stones and clubs. There was only one family of believers in the settlement up to that time, and they insisted that I spend the night in their little hut to keep from serious injury or death. As I left the village very early the next morning, we found that a large ditch had been dug across a strategic part of the road to block our exit. We were able to repair it and I departed.

A little less than a month later, I went back to this village for more meetings. I was met by two Indian women shouting, "We don't want anything you have to offer," and they were hitting me through the open car window as I slowly drove down the road announcing the gospel meetings. I sped up slightly and the women were left running behind my car, still shouting.

After arriving at the run-down, thatch-roofed schoolhouse, we began setting up for the gospel films. We could see Indian huts dotting the mountains on all sides below the breath-taking beauty of the the Andes Mountains. Slowly the Indians made their way down the beautiful rugged mountains that surrounded this lovely valley and soon a large crowd gathered.

The two women who caused the trouble earlier were now trying to get the Indians excited again, but the film started and that settled everyone down. After the first film, I gave a message and the Christian Indians presented special music. Then we showed the second film on the Life of Christ. After another message from God's word, the invitation was given, and 44 Indians knelt to accept Christ as their personal Savior. To my surprise and delight, one of the ladies who had been so opposed to our meeting was kneeling with the others, asking Christ to come into her heart. I almost wept for joy to see young and old alike kneel on the cold, wet ground and pray to receive Christ as Savior. Thank God for the power of the gospel to change lives. The hard places are full of blessings, if the Lord is in it.

A couple of months later, we returned to this same schoolhouse in the valley for a conference. The meetings were to be held high above the schoolhouse on a mountainside where one of the believers lived. The Christians had been told not to have any more meetings at the schoolhouse or their homes would be burned down. Nearby stands a small, lone Catholic church with a tiny store close by. That's all there is on this high dome-like hill. You can see the beautiful valleys and rushing mountain streams on all sides and, in the distance, loom the seemingly eternal mountains. It is a majestic spot, yet the people are steeped in superstition and fear. These poor, humble country people had never heard the truth about Jesus Christ and what He has done for all of us.

At the bottom of the mountain, I got out to examine the freshly dug road that seemed to run almost straight up along the side of the mountain. In places, I was sure I could not make it, so the Indians quickly made the road a little wider. Putting my Land Rover in four-wheel drive, I slowly made my way up the steep mountain road. The road had been built so the meetings could be held far away from the threatening Indians—for our protection as well as for protection of the believers. We encountered little hostility except that some buckets of water were thrown on us.

The public address system broke down that afternoon and we had to do all our inviting by word of mouth. As dusk fell, we were pleasantly surprised to see several hundred Indians trudging up that steep rain-soaked hill to see the gospel films and hear the word of God preached. Even in the rain, these people stood to hear of the true Christ who had come to save them. We had a great meeting that night with no opposition from the unbelievers. The Lord had led us to this beautiful hill to bring hope and salvation to over 50 Indians who stepped out to receive Jesus as their personal Savior.

After the service, the owner of the dingy store invited us in to have a cup of hot cinnamon water and a piece of bread. As we entered the store, our eyes slowly became accustomed to the dim flickering oil lamps. Hanging on the walls were strips of dried meat. Dirty jars filled with sugar, flour, salt and some candy sat on the shelves. It was not much of a selection for the shopper, but these Indians buy only the bare necessities of life. As we drank the delicious drink, we again opened the Bible and explained God's plan of salvation to the leaders of this area.

That next evening, the service was also very well attended. I again showed two gospel films, one of which was on the death, burial and resurrection of Christ. Then I preached and gave the invitation and a man and his son, (among others) came forward to accept Christ. The man told me that he was there the night before just to see the films. His son begged and finally persuaded him to come for the films. After seeing on the screen how Christ died for his sins and hearing the message that to go to heaven he must accept Christ, he made his decision. He was thrilled with his new found faith and so were all the people in the church as this man had been an enemy of the gospel for years.

On almost every trip, when I was ready to return to Quito and to my work in the print shop, some Indians wanted a ride into the city. I had to be very cautious, however, and I always asked how many wanted to go because if I gave my consent, the Indian would show up with all, or part of his large family. Or they would ask me to take a *small* package. I would always ask, "*How* small?" If I said I would take it, they might show up with pigs, chickens or a couple hundred pounds of corn or potatoes. There have been times when the Land Rover was so overloaded that the tires were almost flat. The Indians think there is *always* room either inside or on top of the car. No matter how many wanted to crowd into the Land Rover, if I objected, they assured me they would all fit in!

* *

The mudslide covered the entire roadbed and traffic was backed up along the mountain road. As I walked up the road, many of the people told me I could get through with my four-wheel drive vehicle. After looking at the mudslide and being encouraged by the crowd, I thought I would try to get through.

In the Land Rover with me were Jim and Lee Kingma and their two sons who were in Ecuador to work with HCJB for the summer. This was their first trip to the jungle. I entered the mudslide on the shoulder of the road, but the car kept sliding deep into the mud. The mud was a very thick liquid and the car kept sinking deeper and deeper into the mud until it was even with the window of the Land Rover. The harder I tried to get out, the more I slid into the mud. At this point, Jim and the boys got out on the other side of the Land Rover, climbed on top of the vehicle and jumped to safety. A crowd of people gathered and shouted words of encouragement, but none of them offered to help me because the mud was so deep. I knew if the car ever stopped running, the entire engine and exhaust system would be filled with the soupy black mud. The exhaust sounded like a pot of boiling oil as it escaped through the mud.

A bus driver called to me and asked if I had a log chain. I replied that I did. He told me to get it and he would pull me out. The chain was in a compartment under the driver's seat. I told Lee to put her foot on the accelerator and keep the car running while I got the chain from under my seat. I crawled into the back seat and leaned over the front seat and I was finally able to get the log chain.

As I climbed out of the back of the Land Rover, I sank deep into the mud. All the Ecuadorian observers cheered to see me sink even deeper into the mud as I hooked the chain onto my car and made my way to the bus to hook the chain to the bus. Then I reversed my steps and climbed back into the Land Rover. You can imagine the mud I took back into the car with me! The bus was finally able to pull me out of the mudslide.

I never let the motor die, but I did look under the hood. The radiator fan had thrown mud all over the engine and I couldn't tell one part of the engine from the other. The inside of the Land Rover didn't look much better. I made a real mess! After some time, the road workers were able to make a path through the mud slide and we continued our way to the small jungle church. It was all just a mere inconvenience!

I was concerned about all the mud on the engine, but the next morning the Indian believers said they had something to show me. We went out to the Land Rover and it was "clean as a whistle". They had carried water up from the river and cleaned the entire car inside and out.

The three-day conference was filled with enthusiastic Bible studies, gospel films and preaching during which time we saw six Indians step forward to receive Jesus Christ as their personal Savior. The Indians really appreciated and enjoyed the special music provided by Jim, Lee and their sons, Doug and Kevin. The Sunday morning service was thrilling as we saw the Holy Spirit move in a marvelous way, convicting men and women of sin in their lives and seeing them get right with the Lord and with each other before we partook of the Lord's Supper together. Now, we could understand why Satan put that big landslide in our path to this village.

Chapter 13

Preaching, Teaching and Learning

When we arrived at the tiny Indian village high in the rugged Andes Mountains, it was pouring down rain. The Indians had been trying all day to raise a large tent, but because of the cold wind and heavy rain, it was nearly impossible to do so. Just before nightfall, although it was still raining, all the Indians gathered together and we managed to raise the tent. Even though it was very wet, about 400 Indians came and sat on the ground through the entire service which lasted until after midnight. Straw was then brought and placed on the damp ground inside the tent so that more than 100 Indians who had come a long distance would have a place to sleep.

Because of the location of this village (right at the foot of an eternally snow-capped mountian), it was very cold. Every morning, we found thick ice that had formed on the car and on the tent, and the ground was white with frost. Even in my goose-down sleeping bag, I had to wear all of my clothes and throw my coat over my sleeping bag to keep warm.

The Spirit of God was at work during the three-day conference as we saw nineteen Indians step out to receive Jesus Christ as personal Savior. As usual, the days were filled with Bible studies. Seventeen Indians followed the Lord in baptism, after which we had a precious time around the Lord's table. Many Indians broke down and cried as they confessed their sins and made things right with the Lord.

* *

Singing is a great part of the Quichua worship. The believers love to sing far into the night after the service itself is ended. There are always a lot of singing groups at the conferences. One year, at a particular conference which is held annually in a big tent, with more than 2,000 Indians in attendance, we had 24 singing groups. They all sang and if they were good, the Indians asked for a second number from them. Some of the songs had up to 14 verses and they sang all 14 verses. I couldn't show the gospel films until after midnight. I told the Indians that that was far too late ... we had too many singing groups. I asked them to have half as many singing groups the next year. They agreed with me and promised it would be different next time.

One year later as I arrived for the conference, the leaders came to me and said, "We are going to have a lot of people here from many, many churches." I knew what they were trying to tell me and I asked, "How many singing groups will be coming this year?" They looked at each other and then one of the Indians responded, "Forty-eight!" I told them that would be fine, but that we would have the preaching and films before ten o'clock and then they could sing all night. That's exactly what they did.

I later told the Indians that the greatest strength in the Quichua church is their singing. I also added that the greatest strength is also the greatest weakness in the church. They asked me what I meant. I tried to explain to them that the unsaved Indians are attracted to the meetings because of the singing, but after they were saved, they were content to just sing and not grow in the Lord. The fact that these Indians sang all night long sounds wonderful, but the next day when the Bible was being taught, they were sleeping.

Little did I know as the days of the Bible conference progressed, I would be called upon to preach a funeral service in the middle of the week. Two Quichua Christian young people, a boy and a girl, were killed in a tragic accident.

In Ecuador, they do not enbalm so the deceased must be buried the next day or even the same day—as soon as the death certificate is filed. In Ecuador, they do not go through a mortuary to bury a loved one—they simply go to the casket store and choose the casket they want. The family prepares the body and places it in the casket and then, they take their loved one to the cemetery. They *do* have to arrange with the cemetery to have a hole dug. Many times the back of a pick-up truck serves as a hearse to take the body to the cemetery. I have even taken a few caskets in the back of my vheicle.

This was the first time I had ever had a funeral service during a Bible conference. This occasion caused a real awakening among the Quichua Indians as I explained to them that death can come at any time and we had the proof right in front of us. As a result, 77 Indians accepted the Lord as their personal Savior.

The Indians in this area were known as drunkards before they accepted Christ. At one time, it was nearly impossible to drive down the road on a weekend because of the drunk Indians lying all over the road. The wife would sit beside her husband and spin wool until he woke up and then she tried to get him home. The wives made sure that their hats were on their heads at all times! That seemed to be very important. Sometimes the men wore two hats. They wore the old hat over the new one to keep the new one clean. When they reached the town or village, they put the new hat on top of the old one. Everyone, men, women and children wore felt hats. In the church services, every hat came off in respect to God and His Word. Even the unsaved had this respect.

After these Indians accepted the Lord and quit spending all their money on liquor, they had money to build better homes. Most of them now live in cement block homes and have bottled gas stoves on which to cook.

The unsaved Indians started saying that the missionaries were buying the souls of the Christians and that is why they had so much money. One Indian pastor told me that two young women came to him and told him they wanted to sell their souls. The pastor asked them how much they wanted for their souls. The girls came up with a price and the pastor agreed and said, "I have the money, but first you have to give me your soul." The girls asked, "How do we do that?" The pastor replied, " You are selling your soul to me, but don't even know how to give it to me." Then the pastor presented Christ to them and they both accepted Christ without receiving *any* money. They received something **far better** than money!

* *

I went to one meeting, a Bible conference in a different part of the mountains, and was there for a whole week, showing films and preaching every night. By the end of the week, I was finally getting pretty worn out. The last night, an incredibly filthy little boy latched onto me. He hung around me and kept putting his hands on me. The boy obviously had a headcold and no handkerchief was evident, except his hand and sleeves. I finally couldn't stand it any longer and told the boy to go to the faucet and wash his hands, but to no avail. After a couple times of urging the boy to wash, I began to get irritated. About that time the local Indian pastor came up to me and asked me if I would give the last message of the conference with only five minutes notice.

I knew that the Indians didn't understand subtle and oblique words—they have to be told everything directly. So I got up and preached a message on cleanliness, how only God could make us clean inside. Then I went on and talked about personal cleanliness, and I told them, "You go out in the field all day and you work, you sweat and your body stinks. You go home and *maybe* you go down to the river and *maybe* you even wash, but then you put the same dirty clothes back on and you still stink."

By this time I was getting into it! So I went a little further. "When you get on a bus, do you know why no one wants to sit by you and you end up alone at the back of the bus? It's not because you are an Indian! No! It's because you stink!" Then I thought, "Man, what am I doing? I'm probably really getting into hot water here!" But I went ahead and finished the message. After I was finished and sat down, the local pastor stood up and said, "Oh beloved! We just want to thank Brother Schroder for that precious message tonight!"

I could hardly believe what I heard! "Precious"? I had just blasted these poor people for being dirty, and it was called, "a precious message"?

So when I went back to Quito, I looked up my good friend, Jose Naula, probably the most famous preacher in all Ecuador among the Quichua Indians. "Why would that pastor say my message was *precious*?" I asked Jose. And I told him what I had said in my sermon.

Jose answered,"Oh if you told them that, they liked it because they like it direct. They *really* liked it! They thought, 'Boy now, that guy really loves us to tell it to us straight like that.'"

I then learned that you have to hit them straight on. You don't hint around. I even got requests to repeat that same message in other villages.

* *

An Indian believer said to me, "We can make a hole in the mud wall, so you can drive right up to my house." This seemed like an awfully big job since the mud walls are about two feet thick, but many Indians with large hoes quickly made the opening we needed to get through. I drove through the open field to the Indian's home. The believer was not satisfied with my car being left overnight in a field for fear of what may happen to it, so they quickly made openings in two more mud walls just wide enough for the car to enter into their yard.

As nightfall came, we announced the meetings over the loud speakers. Indians began to arrive until nearly 200 were squeezed into the believer's yard. We had groups of singers from visiting Indian villages and two gospel films were shown. After my message, seven Indians came forward to accept Jesus Christ as their personal Savior. The singing continued until after midnight.

Cutting through the wall reminded me of another meeting I was holding accompanied by my son, Tod. We had the car safely inside the believer's yard through a hole they made in the wall. The meetings were going well, but one afternoon the unsaved Indians began to harass the believers. Tod was next to a mud wall, when I saw two of the unsaved Indians sneaking up on the other side of the wall. I knew they were after him, so I shouted in English, "Tod, run! And don't look back!" He did as I told him and at the same time the unsaved Indians jumped up and reached over the wall to grab him. He just barely got away in time.

The next morning, one of the Indians came to tell me that during the night antagonistic Indians had torn out the bridge which was the only way we could get out to the main road. In spite of this preoccupation, we continued with the meetings for that Sunday morning. Eight Indians gave their testimonies and I baptized them in a hole they dug in the ground and filled with water. After the baptismal service, all the Christians participated in the Lord's Supper.

I got very little sleep the night before. The Indians gave me a bed to sleep on but it was too short for me. I couldn't stretch out. After fighting it for hours, I decided to sleep on the floor with the guinea pigs. I just hoped they didn't eat my sleeping bag, or even worse, try to get in the sleeping bag with me.

The next morning, we all walked down to examine the damage to the bridge. Since there was no opposition at the bridge site, the Christians began to rebuild the bridge and we left almost on schedule.

* *

After I had been traveling three hours through the breath-taking beauty of the Andes Mountains, I finally reached the summit of the pass, at an altitude of 14,000 feet. I then began the descent to what the Ecaudorians call the coast, even though it is several hours drive from the Pacific Ocean.

As I dropped down from the lofty heights of the Andes Mountains, I soon began to feel the balmy, humid air of this coastal area. Banana trees became a familiar sight and the tropical fruits sold by local farmers appeared in front of their bamboo houses. These bamboo houses are all quite open, perched on top of stilts to allow air to circulate and to protect them from wild animals.

Many Quichua Indians moved out of the high mountain area because of lack of land to be cultivated. I went to minister to these people. I was warmly welcomed by the Quichua believers and told that even though they listened regularly to HCJB, no missionary ever visited their church before.

The church was small and we all agreed that the films and preaching should be done in the open air. Because they expected many Spanish-speaking people, I was asked to bring the message. Nearly 300 people filled the street. There were people peering out of very window, door, nook and cranny. When the invitation was given, 15 people responded to accept the Lord as their personal Savior.

I made only a few trips to the coastal area since I worked mainly with the Quichua Indians and there were very few of them on the coast as compared to more mountainous parts of Ecuador.

That night I was given a place to sleep and about midnight, I felt something crawling all over me. I got my flashlight and saw hundreds of fleas crawling all over my body. I never got bit, but I couldn't stand having those critters all over me, so I got up, shook out my sleeping bag and went to sleep in the car. It wasn't a good night.

* * * * * * * * * * * * * * * * * * * *

The air was hot and muggy the night I arrived in Lago Agrio, deep in the Ecuadorian jungle, after traveling ten hours over bumpy, dusty roads.

Pedro Grefa was the pastor of the three churches which I had helped to organize in that region. Pedro invited me to his wedding. I was the best man in the first Christian wedding in that area. Being the best man meant that I had to pay for the entire wedding. It is a great honor, but one doesn't want that honor too often.

The wedding was held in an open-ended bamboo building which served as a church. An arch of palm branches entwined with wild flowers adorned the front of the rustic building where the couple stood during the ceremony.

Pedro's bride, who was ten years younger than he, was dressed in a gown of white satin. This was not a common sight in this area, thus creating quite a bit of interest. It is very customary, however, for an Ecuadorian man to marry a girl ten to twelve years younger than himself.

With hundreds of Indians and Latins in attendance, the ceremony began with congregational singing, accompanied by guitars. Then I gave a short message. The marriage ceremony was beautiful. Another missionary friend of Pedro's was in charge of the ceremony. After the ceremony an invitation was given and five people accepted Christ as their personal Savior.

The wedding dinner was attended by all present. The menu consisted of chicken, soup, rice, eggs, cooked roots of plants and boiled bananas. It was a wonderful experience. Pedro and I worked together for several years before his marriage and we continued ministering throughout the jungle after his marriage. I was thrilled when they named their first son after me.

As I said earlier, I do not like the jungle because it is hot, humid, full of bugs, snakes and everything I do not like, but God led me to help in the establishment of several churches deep in the jungle.

The Oyacachi church sent some of their believers to start three churches along the road to Lago Agrio. I was privileged to minister alongside these brethren by holding special meetings and helping the HCJB medical caravans that went to these churches.

On one trip with my son, Tod, we encountered many problems. First, we had to wait a whole day for a landslide to be cleared. Then our portable power plant quit on us. It was frozen solid. That meant a complete overhaul, rings, pistons and all. We were able to borrow another generator, just after finding out that we had blown out one of our speakers. Later that night, the projector completely ate up one of our Gospel films. That had never happened to us before and it never happened again. The Indians wanted to help us pack up and one of them pulled the light bulb straight out of the socket—the socket and the bulb. He told me, "I thought it was really hard to get out." On top of that, the tailgate on the car got sprung because so many Indians stood on it. But we praised the Lord for the 30 Indians who accepted the Lord. All that equipment could be fixed. We rejoiced in the thought that even one soul was worth it all.

* *

Felix was a drunkard and a cattle thief, but while working on the dam at Loreto with us, he accepted the Lord and was baptized in Lake Loreto. His changed life was a real testimony to his family and his entire community. Monnie and I visited his humble home high in the Andes Mountains. His mother, father and younger brother made their decisions for Christ also.

Felix fell in love with a young Indian girl, Rosario, whom he wanted to marry. Felix knew that the Bible was clear about not marrying an unsaved person, so he brought her into Quito to the print shop to talk to me. After an hour or so, she made her decision to accept Christ. Then about two months later, they came back to the print shop to talk again. Felix would not marry her unless she was baptized. Since they did not belong to any church, I arranged to baptize her in a fishpond at a missionary's home in Quito. The pond was only a couple of feet deep so I almost had to lay her out flat to baptize her.

Monnie and I offered to have the wedding in our home. We asked Felix and Rosario how many of their relatives and friends would be coming. They told us there would be about twenty.

The afternoon, before the wedding, Monnie and I cleared most of the furniture out of the living room and set up chairs which were loaned to us by HCJB. Monnie had a cake made for the occasion and she prepared lots of small sandwiches, cheese cubes with a tooth pick in each one and popped some corn. She purchased Spanish peanuts and chocolate candy which was wrapped in brightly colored paper. We also made coffee and had juice to drink. We were all ready for the wedding. Ruth and Joe Baxter were to sing and J. D. Clark, a veteran missionary statesman, was to preach a message and perform the ceremony. Monnie and I would be standing up with the bride and groom.

Late in the afternoon, the Indians began to arrive. Since it was market day in Quito, they had taken advantage of their trip into the capital city to attend the market. They came to our house with chickens, pigs and even a sheep. We had to put our two dogs in the washhouse to keep them from killing and eating the chickens and chasing the pigs and the sheep. The Indians kept coming, and coming. We planned for twenty guests, but by the time they arrived, there were sixty guests who showed up at our front door. Monnie was beside herself.

Just then the door bell rang, again. Standing there was a very well-dressed Ecuadorian man and his wife and they asked, "Is this where the Indian wedding is being held?" Monnie responded, "Yes." They asked if they could attend the wedding. We invited them in and asked them to be seated. The lady, sensing Monnie's dilemma of having not prepared for so many unexpected guests, began to help her by cutting the cheese and sandwiches in small pieces. When we were ready to serve, she organized a line (which the Indians are not accustomed to) and as they passed by the table, she cut the cake in small pieces so everyone could have a piece. We sent our children to the corner store to purchase more candy and peanuts, and we popped more corn.

The wedding was a real testimony to all the Indians who came, but Monnie nearly "lost it". The Indians, who were used to having guinea pigs as garbage disposals, spit the husks from the peanuts (and anything else that was not to their satisfaction) on the floor . They threw the toothpicks and candy wrappers on the floor and wiped their hands on the drapes—they had no idea of how a paper napkin was to be used. Many of them spilled punch on the floor. With sixty Quichua Indians (who seldom bathe) in a closed house, you can imagine what the smell must have been. To say the least, Monnie was not too happy with that situation.

While I took some of the Indians back to their mountain homes, Monnie, our children and the Baxters opened all the windows and started cleaning the house. The Ecuadorian couple disappeared as quickly as they had come, without even telling us goodbye. Monnie maintains to this day that God sent her an angel to help with the serving at the wedding reception. Maybe so, but in any case, we determined that the next wedding would be in the mountains far from our home.

Chapter 14

Time Waits for No One

Through the years, I thrilled to see what God was doing among the Quichua Indians in the highlands of Ecuador. When we began working with them, the new believers were strong in the faith and could not be shaken even under persecution, but something began to happen.

We started to get second and third generation Christians who were saved, but not out of lives of deep sin. They had never had to put their lives on the line for their faith. Some of these younger believers wanted to dabble a little bit in sin just to see what it was all about.

Some had enough money to make a down payment on a truck. They *said* they would use it for the Lord, but the only day they could make money with the truck was on market day, which was always Sunday. The men also started traveling into the city and they observed how nicely dressed the women were in the city. They realized that these women dressed differently and *smelled* differently than the sweaty, smoke-saturated wife they left at home. Some of them became discontent and left their wives.

Also, as the years passed, electricity came to many villages along the road and that meant the Indians could purchase television sets. The good programs always were shown on Sunday nights and that made some stay away from the church services. Others wanted to change the world using political powers. All in all, these things, this so-called progress, was sad to see and we knew they needed to grow in the Lord sufficiently to overcome these outward attractions that Satan had to offer.

Now, we were seeing a different kind of attack from the enemy. Oh, yes, some were still stoned and suffered at the hands of the hostile unsaved, but the attacks that the devil was throwing at many of them were much more subtle and inviting.

Sometimes, I told the Indians in a meeting, "I wish about 500 hostile Indians would attack this group of 'so-called believers' just to see how many of you are 'true believers.'" In spite of all this, God is *truly* building His Church among the Quichua Indians. It is marvelous to behold. What a blessing to have been used of the Lord to minister among these dear beloved people.

* *

In June of 1983, the president of HCJB World Radio, Ron Cline, asked Monnie and me if we would be willing to return to the United States and do representation work. Our first response was "No", but we agreed to pray about it.

As we prayed about the move, we began to see God leading in that direction. I didn't want to leave the work I was doing among the Quichua Indians. However, there were many Quichua pastors now, and they were very capable of doing the work themselves. I also realized that many times the Quichuas asked me to preach just because I was there. They could have held the meetings without me. Over the years, we had seen some veteran missionaries discourage and run off new missionaries just because they were fearful of losing their positions. They sometimes built a hedge around their job and ministry and attacked anyone who came near—often not even realizing what they were doing. Monnie and I had prayed we would never allow this to happen with us.

My major responsibility at the mission, the print shop, had capable men to run it as well and perhaps God *was* giving us a new ministry in answer to our prayers. It was a hard decision, so we wrote to all of our supporters and asked them to pray with us.

People always say it doesn't cost anything to pray. I jokingly say, "If you really don't want to do something, don't pray about it because you can be sure that God will lead you into that very thing!" In December of 1983, after 23 years of exciting, wonderful ministry for the Lord in Ecuador, we said tearful goodbyes to our many Quichua Indian believers, Ecuadorian friends and missionary colleagues, and returned to the States to serve Him here in a new and different ministry.

* *

Let me ask you a question. "Are you willing to give up your life for Christ?" Maybe you can say "Yes", and if you really mean it, praise the Lord! But perhaps you say "Yes" because you have never faced the real possibility of dying in the service of Christ. I had to face this question one day in my ministry.

In the space of a few months, I experienced the following: I was attacked by 300 to 400 Indians, the road was cut many times, we had to build a bridge to escape the enemy, I was threatened and called all kinds of names, was shot at, saw men around me beaten almost to death. My car was damaged with clubs, rocks were thrown at me, I saw Christian Indian's homes burned to the ground and my son was almost captured by the enemy. Now word came to me that the meeting I was to have the next night was in a very dangerous place. The unsaved Indians from 13 communities held demonstrations and threatened to kill all the believers, especially the missionary.

Then I asked myself, "Am I really ready to die for Christ?"

That is when I thought of lots of reasons not to go. I had a *family* and I must care for them. Maybe I could go *another time.* Perhaps my going would make it *worse* for the Christian Indians. I was also getting *too old.* By now the national *church* should be doing this work. Besides, the *sleeping conditions* are not good and the *food* is even worse. Most of all, if I should die, who would do my *work*? These were just some of the reasons (on the human side of me) which went rushing through my mind—all good reasons not to go.

Still not being convinced, I asked others what I should do. Some of the missionaries told me not to go; still others said they didn't know what I should do, but they would pray for me. One of my workers in the print shop said he would go with me, but when I explained the details, he backed out, saying his father was very ill. Another one of my workers said he would go, but when I asked him who would care for his wife and five children if he was killed, he said, "Maybe I shouldn't go."

Why are we not willing to die for Christ? Sometimes it is fear of the unknown or fear of getting hurt. I always said, "I am ready to die for Christ, but I don't want to just get hurt."

Sometimes Christians love the comforts of home too much and are unwilling to give them up. I have said to Monnie, "I want the best, most comfortable and nicest home we can have as long as it does not keep me from going out to reach the Indians."

Sometimes it is the cares of this world. We just have so many *other things* that fill our lives, we have no time for Christ. It is stated quite well in Philipians 2:21, *"For all seek their own, not the things which are of Christ."* And Matthew 15:8 says, *"This people draweth nigh unto me with their mouth and honoreth me with their lips but the heart is far from me."*

If that is true, then what makes one ready and willing to lay down his life for Christ? I believe the bottom line is a deep desire to please God and win souls. Proverbs 11:30, *"He that winneth souls is wise."* Our life is not our own. It belongs to God. Why are we so attached to it?

Well, the flesh told me not to go to this village and I had lots of reasons not to go, but I knew I must go. Why did I have to go? I couldn't let these believers down and I knew if I didn't go this time

I would be scared out forever. I told Monnie, "We just can't yield to the threats of the unsaved. If these believers can put their lives on the line for Christ every day, and I can't put my life on the line for one night, I am not worthy to be called a missionary."

I told the Christian Indian who called to call me back the next day and I would tell him if I would come or not. When he called the next morning, I told him we would be there. I didn't know who "we" would be. Shortly after that, my friend (who was a pastor from the southern part of Ecuador) came into the print shop to see me and I told me him about the trip. He told me he would like to go with me.

We left Quito and traveled on the Pan-American highway, eventually turning off on a dirt road that led to the Indian village. I stopped the car at the crossroads and said to Manuel, "You have a wife and two young children. What would happen to them if you get killed tonight?" He replied, "God will take care of them." I told him that once we started up that mountain road, we were going all the way. "Let's go," he said.

Did we have fears? Yes! I guess we had some fears of the unknown and some doubts, but we both had the peace of God that we were doing the right thing.

When we arrived at the small church there was already a large crowd assembled. We set up the equipment and had our service as planned. There were many more Indians than we had expected, and so far there had been no trouble. The trouble usually comes after the service, anyway. All the Indians had heard about the threats, but they came anyway. Some may have just come to see the excitement, but when I gave the invitation to accept Christ, 21 Indians came forward to ask Christ into their hearts.

As we packed up for the trip home, we wondered if we would be allowed back down the narrow mountain road or if we would be met by a group of antagonistic Indians. We encountered no problems at all! God was **testing us** to see just how far we would go with Him. He was with us **every step of the way.** What a blessing we would have lost if we had refused to follow His leading.

Are you willing to give your life for Christ—to follow His leading wherever it takes you, to live boldly for Him each day?

The cause is great -

the rewards are eternal -

the blessing is sure -

and the fields are ripe.

Are you willing?